W9-BSV-910

5697

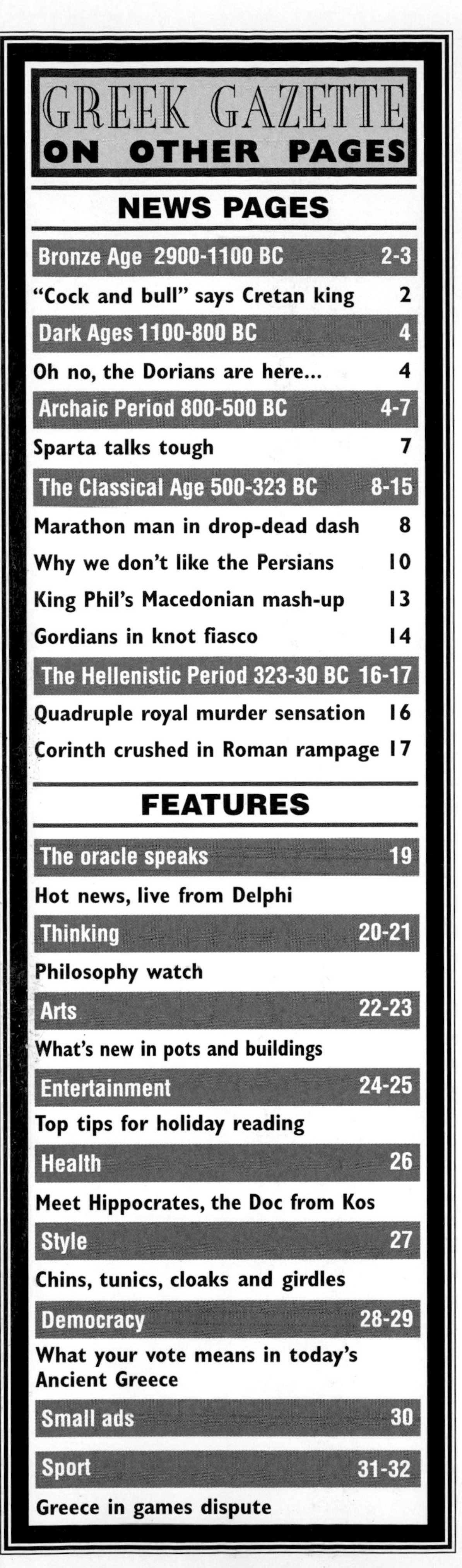

GREEK GAZETTE ON OTHER PAGES

NEWS PAGES

FEATURES

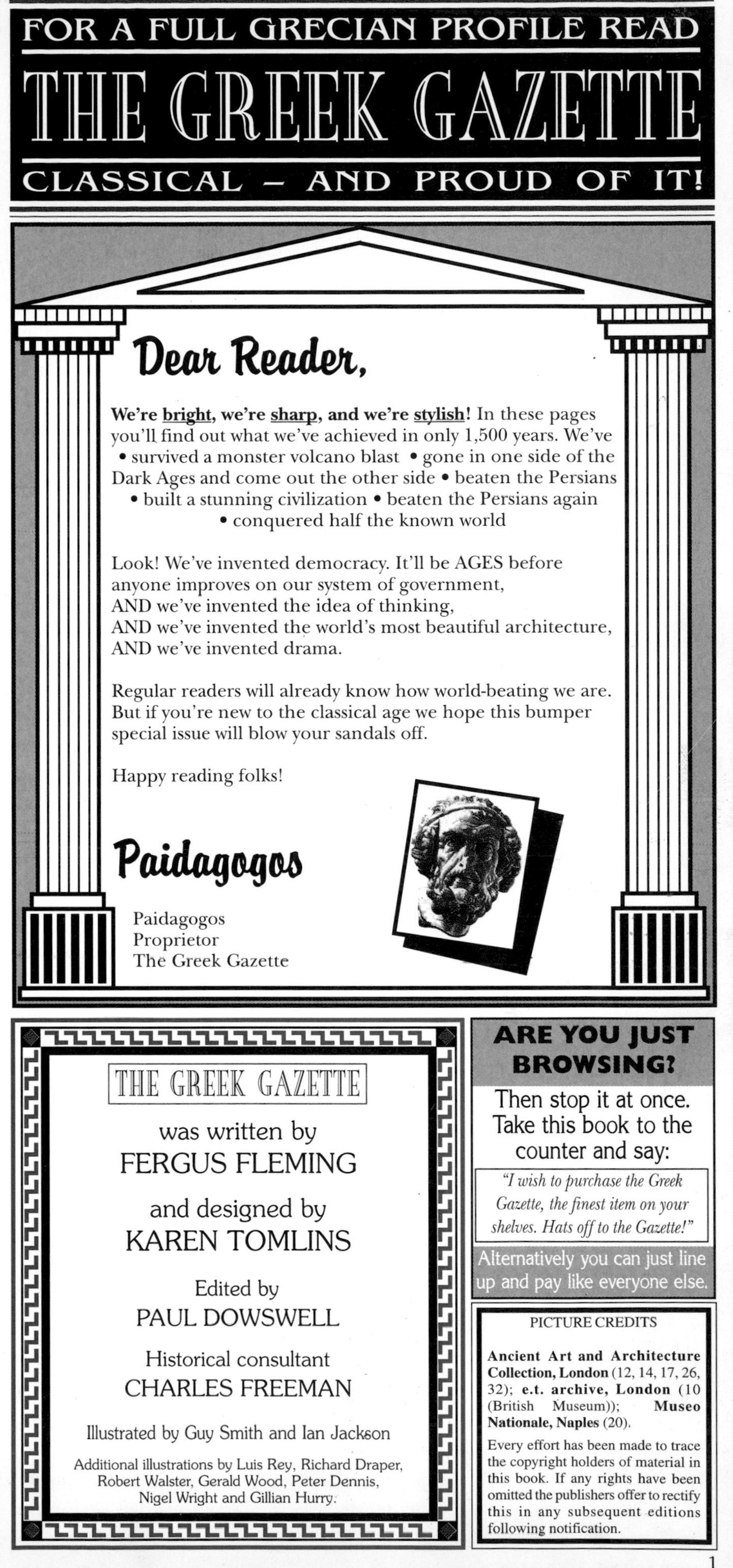

FOR A FULL GRECIAN PROFILE READ

THE GREEK GAZETTE

CLASSICAL – AND PROUD OF IT!

Dear Reader,

We're <u>bright</u>, we're <u>sharp</u>, and we're <u>stylish</u>! In these pages you'll find out what we've achieved in only 1,500 years. We've
• survived a monster volcano blast • gone in one side of the Dark Ages and come out the other side • beaten the Persians • built a stunning civilization • beaten the Persians again • conquered half the known world

Look! We've invented democracy. It'll be AGES before anyone improves on our system of government,
AND we've invented the idea of thinking,
AND we've invented the world's most beautiful architecture,
AND we've invented drama.

Regular readers will already know how world-beating we are. But if you're new to the classical age we hope this bumper special issue will blow your sandals off.

Happy reading folks!

Paidagogos

Paidagogos
Proprietor
The Greek Gazette

THE GREEK GAZETTE

was written by
FERGUS FLEMING

and designed by
KAREN TOMLINS

Edited by
PAUL DOWSWELL

Historical consultant
CHARLES FREEMAN

Illustrated by Guy Smith and Ian Jackson

Additional illustrations by Luis Rey, Richard Draper, Robert Walster, Gerald Wood, Peter Dennis, Nigel Wright and Gillian Hurry.

ARE YOU JUST BROWSING?

Then stop it at once. Take this book to the counter and say:

"I wish to purchase the Greek Gazette, the finest item on your shelves. Hats off to the Gazette!"

Alternatively you can just line up and pay like everyone else.

PICTURE CREDITS

Ancient Art and Architecture Collection, London (12, 14, 17, 26, 32); **e.t. archive, London** (10 (British Museum)); **Museo Nationale, Naples** (20).

1600 BC

Crete King in Knossos Kontroversy

Theseus, the King of Athens, has fallen out with the King of Knossos following a dramatic visit to Crete – the island headquarters of Minoan civilization.

"I'd heard they were sacrificing Greek boys and girls to a monster, so I went there to kill it," said the hunky hero. "When I reached the capital, Knossos, I realized they needed some radical pest control. There was this big maze called a Labyrinth which contained a dreadful monster called a Minotaur. It was like a man but with a bull's head. And to keep it happy the Minoans fed it little Greek children.

"'Well,' I thought. 'This won't do.' So I went in and killed it and brought out its head as proof."

Thongs off to Theseus!

OUTRAGE

But the King of Knossos tells a different story.

"It's all a legend!" cried the outraged monarch. "This Greek peasant came in smelling of goats and got completely lost in our palace with all its rooms and corridors. He only thinks it's a labyrinth because he hasn't seen anything larger than an outdoor toilet. And as for the so-called Minotaur. Well! Everybody knows that's nonsense. What happens is that I wear a bull's mask during certain rituals because the bull is our national symbol.

"The fact of the matter is that the Greeks are jealous of what we've achieved here on Crete." The King is right. The Minoans have:

- ***big palaces***
- ***excellent water supply and drainage systems***
- ***whole storerooms of large earthenware jars crammed with food, oil and wine***
- ***an indecipherable form of writing called Linear A***
- ***and a frightening national sport called bull-leaping in which you grab a charging bull by the horns and flip yourself over its back.***

"The Greeks don't have anything like this," said the King. "Pah! They'll never be a classical civilization."

A *Gazette* artist recreates Theseus's account of his showdown with the Minotaur. Guess who won!

The little island of Thera gave the Minoans a nasty shock yesterday. It blew up – and completely destroyed their civilization!

In an astonishing display of vitality, Thera transformed itself from a nice round island with a mountain in the middle into a large bay surrounded by a crescent-shaped piece of land and the odd rock sticking out above water.

"At first we thought it was a domestic accident," said one member of the emergency services. "But it proved to be the biggest volcanic eruption this millenium. Apparently the island was a dormant volcano. We don't know what set it off.

"However, preliminary investigations have ruled out arson."

HAVOC

The explosion caused havoc on Crete, which is only 110km (70 miles) away from Thera. Wearing only his nightshirt the King of Knossos gave his version of events.

"Last night the royal slumber was disturbed by the noise of earth tremors, massive tidal waves and widespread flooding. When I opened the window to complain I saw that the crops had been destroyed, the city had fallen down and our entire civilization had been wiped out."

His Majesty admits that Crete is no longer a major player in the Mediterranean.

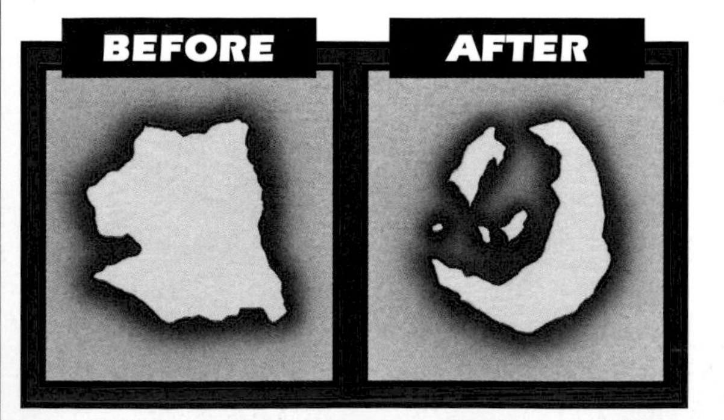

Experts think a faulty gas oven is probably not to blame.

MYCE-'N-EASY DOES IT!

GREEKS COME ACROP-OLIS!!

1450 BC

Who's who in Greece? The Mycenaeans, that's who. Nobody's quite sure where they came from, but they're the top dogs now. From their headquarters at Mycenae, they've set up settlements all over the country and have even conquered the Minoans.

"We may be just a rag-taggle of tribes," said a Mycenaean spokesman, "but we're skilled marauders and our culture has spread throughout Greece and beyond. We've founded strongholds like Athens and Thebes, and introduced our language and gods to the locals. We've even captured Knossos."

"The greatest thing we've done, though, is to introduce a new form of writing. On Crete they used Linear A which no one could understand apart from them. We've gone one better. We're calling ours Linear B. In the future people will look at Linear A and say, 'What a lot of meaningless squiggles!' Then they'll come to Linear B and say, 'Thank goodness! At last some writing that makes sense.'

"What's more, we've invented a whole new way of fortifying our towns. What we do is find a piece of high ground, surround it with a massive wall, and call it an acropolis. When people try to invade, we just hit them with swords and tell them to go away. And they do. Amazing!"

The *Gazette* says, "This is where Greek civilization really gets into its swing."

Now that we're more civilized we've got time to engage in idle pursuits, such as painting an octopus on the side of a pot.

TROJANS SLIP IN HORSE BUSINESS

1250 BC

Greeks make hay as Trojans whine

When Paris, Prince of Troy, ran off with beautiful Princess Helen of Greece he couldn't have made a worse mistake. King "Angry" Agamemnon sent his entire fleet to get her back.

"We besieged Troy for ten years and lost a lot of good men," said Angry at a press conference yesterday. "We were at our wits' end. But then we came up with a winning tactic. We pretended to run away and leave them a large wooden horse by way of saying sorry."

"Just what we always wanted!" thought the Trojans. They saw the Greeks had gone, and dragged the horse into town. But what they didn't realize was that the Greeks had only run away behind the nearest hill and that the horse was hollow and filled with elite troops.

When night fell the soldiers crept out of the horse, seized the town and opened the gates to let the Greek army in. They massacred half the population and turned the rest into slaves. No-one got away apart from a warrior named Aeneas, who escaped after having had most of his consonants removed.

Horse sense. The Trojans obviously didn't have any.

TOP POETS IN FACT FLAP

In a shock announcement, the Troy and Associated Ports Press Council (TRAPPCO) has slammed the accuracy of Greek reporting.

"Yes, the Trojan War did take place. No, it wasn't anything like Greek papers say it was," claimed a TRAPPCO spokesman. "What happened was that some minor Mycenaean lords destroyed the major trading city of Troy. But they didn't take ten years over it. And there was no Helen, no Paris and most certainly no wooden horse.

"The entire story has been invented by the Greek bards in order to glorify their country's achievements. Like Homer, for instance. In the past this man has published a number of misleading articles. Everyone knows his so-called epic *The Odyssey* – about some fellow who slays a one-eyed monster, oh, and something about a wicked witch who turns people into animals... What a fable that turned out to be!"

The Greek press angrily rejected the slur but TRAPPCO wasn't backing down.

"History will prove us right. You'll see."

The Dorians Are Here!

"We're washed up!" In an exclusive interview Mycenaean peasant Totali Yatolos tells the *Gazette* how Greek civilization fell.

"Things were bad, I've got to admit. It started off with a string of poor harvests. Then it got to food shortages. And the next thing we knew it was famine.

"Those who could get out did. Apparently they've been roaming the Mediterranean, looting and raiding. As for the rest of us, we stayed put and fought between ourselves. That's when we noticed we'd been taken over by the Dorians."

So exactly who are the Dorians? "Nobody knows where we come from," a prominent Dorian told us helpfully. "In fact some people even think we're Greeks. As far as we're concerned civilization is finished. There's going to be no more Bronze Age, no more cities, no more trade.

OUTRAGE

"From now on it's all hard times and not much to eat. **We're nomads and we think everyone else should be.** We're going to be grazing their fields like there's no tomorrow. Oh yes. And because the art of writing has been lost we can do **what we like when we like** and there will be no records. Brilliant!"

Mr. Yatalos disagrees, but he's in no position to say so.

JUST LOOK WHAT THEY'VE DONE TO OUR POTS!!!

Before the Dorians

Clever, lively figures. Bright, varied glazes.

What we've got now

Muddy, brown stickmen. Call THAT art!?!

WE'VE REALLY VOWELLED UP

800 BC

It's official! Greek is the world's first written language to have vowels.

"We've really grabbed the ancient world by its ears," said Professor of Alphabets, Demi Mouros. "Like all great inventions it looks simple. But it's been quite a complicated process."

It all started when Prof. Mouros's team of Athenian experts studied a consonants-only alphabet used by Phoenician traders. They soon realized there was room for improvement.

"We noticed that the Phoenicians left it up to the reader to fill in the vowels. But this obviously wasn't good enough. Looking at some of their bills we noticed it was impossible to tell if they were invoicing for a cargo of sacks or a cargo of socks. Well, that's not quite true because we don't wear socks and we don't use sacks. But you get my drift. So we looked at ways of making things clearer. That's when we hit on the idea of vwls."

In a session of brainstorming the linguists came up with a range of noises to suit any occasion.

"We started off with five vowels –a, e, i, o and u. But then we thought we'd add a few more, in case of emergencies. As a result, Greek now boasts seven vowels which we call alpha, epsilon, eta, iota, omicron, upsilon and omega. That's α, ε, η, ι, ο, υ and ω."

"Using them's easy. All you do is insert them between the consonants. For example, take the word crpls. Looks bizarre doesn't it? But just add a few vowels and Bingo! You've got acropolis."

"Of course, there have been one or two teething problems. Troublemakers have started inventing words which are almost all consonants with hardly any vowels at all – apophthegm, for example, which means a general truth." What a mouthful! We're advising anyone who comes across such a word to use a combination of simpler ones which everyone can understand."

Greeks are going crazy over the new alphabet. Many people can read and write it. And they're using it for all kinds of wacky purposes, like scrawling their names on pots. Some people have even started to write poems.

Major rulers, however, are furious. In their trade journal, *Ff Wth Thr Hds*, they have made it clear that they disapprove of the new development.

"It's disgraceful," said the King of Corinth. "**Before long people will be saying exactly what they like. Outrageous**!"

Vowels unveiled yesterday by Professor Mouros. Oracles predict a bright future for a,e,i,o and u, but not ω and η.

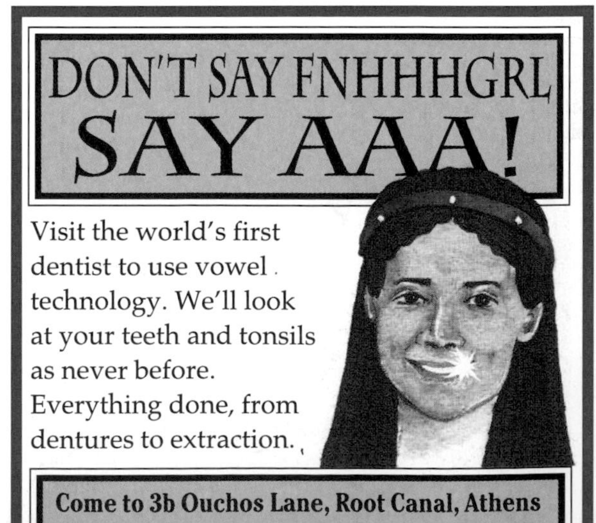

POLIS-ED TO MEET YOU!

"GOATS ARE OFF!" SAY CITIZENS

FRIEZE – IT'S THE POLIS! Not a frieze at all in fact, but an illustration by a *Gazette* artist.

700 BC

It's goodbye Dark Ages and hello civilization as Greece goes city-state crazy! Throughout the land people are forming states with their own aristocratic rulers, their own farmland and above all their own cities. They're so pleased with their new way of life they've given it a name – the polis.

"We got the idea from the east – places like Phoenicia and Turkey," said one satisfied aristo. "There they were with big, fortified cities, prosperous agriculture and sophisticated trade networks. And there we were thinking, 'Ho-hum. Centuries of squalor lie ahead. If only we were like those guys in Asia Minor.' Then we realized: 'Hey! What have they got that we haven't? Nothing!' So we decided to copy them."

OUTRAGE

City-state mania is sweeping Greece. Places like Sparta, Corinth and Thebes are already classed as major-league polises. And hundreds of other newcomers are emerging.

As for the Dorians?

"Now and then you find some raggedy nomad trying to graze a herd of goats on polis land. **We just tell him to get lost.**"

POLIS FILE

Can you tell a polis from a hole in the ground? The *Gazette* gives you ten facts on the most wanted life in Ancient Greece.

- Size – unimportant. It's what you do with it that counts. Can range from Athens's 2,500 square km (1,000 square miles) to the island of Chios which supports four polises on an area one-third of the size.
- City – vital. Every polis must have one.
- Fields – very important. Otherwise everyone would starve.
- Agora – marketplace. Hub of the city.
- Acropolis – fortified citadel. Hide here when someone attacks.
- Temple – dedicated to patron deity.
- Citizens – a must. Status usually hereditary.
- Slaves – essential. Otherwise citizens would have no free time.
- Metics – foreigners. Bring in valuable trade. Not allowed to be citizens.
- Army – well, farmers with swords actually. Useful for fighting other polises on dull days.

ARISTOS TOLD TO "HOP-LITE" OFF

They were jabbin' and a stabbin' at the Hop (lite).

650 BC

Polis life is being given a shake-up as Greek rulers are told: Toe the line or get out.

"We're sick and tired of them," said an outraged citizen. "They go around with their noses in the air, tax us heavily and take all the food when there's a famine. We haven't been able to do anything about it in the past because they've got horses and chariots and can just ride us down. **But now we've got a secret weapon they can't beat – the hoplite!**"

Hoplites are the hottest new items in warfare. Heavily-armed infantrymen with shields and long spears, they form themselves into a long formation called a phalanx which the cavalry can't dent.

"It's terrible," complained one ex-king. "We invented the hoplites to fight wars for us. But now if we don't do what they want they throw us out and put some ghastly man called a tyrant in charge. If you ask me, Greek civilization is going downhill."

Being a tyrant has become the most popular job in Greece. Everyone with any clout wants the position and if they can't find an aristo to depose they chuck out another tyrant.

"Beats farming, which is what we'd be doing otherwise," said a hoplite. "And it's great fun. When you've got two armies facing up to each other it's **Godzilla-meets-King-Kong stuff**. Some people say they want proper laws and that. **But between you and me, we all need a little mayhem really.**"

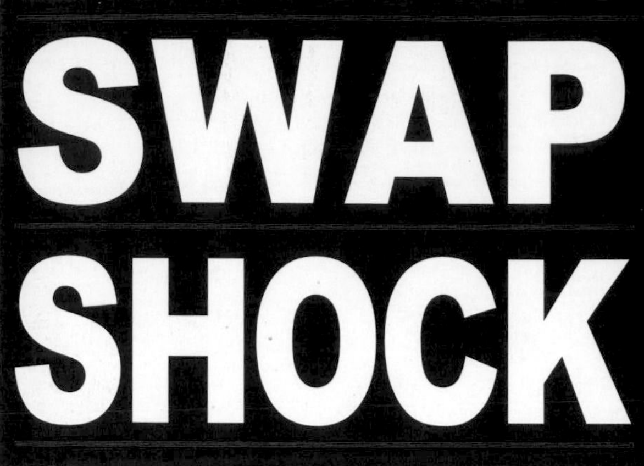

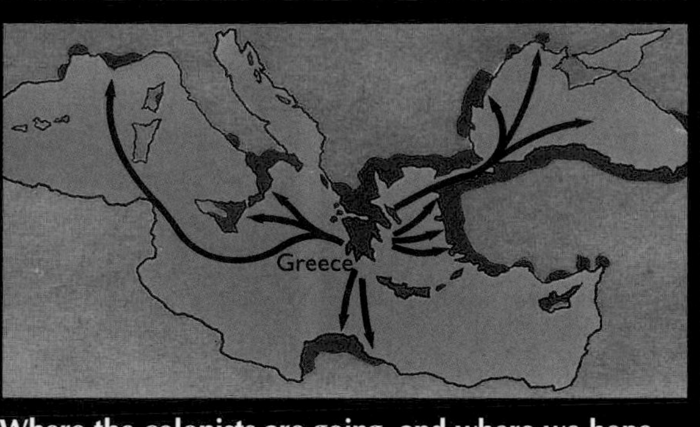

Where the colonists are going, and where we hope most of them will stay.

Desperate Dan Delion, a colonist from Corinth, has made the worst deal of the century. He and some pals rowed a boat to Sicily intending to grab some land and parcel it out between them. But on the way his food ran out and he was so hungry that he swapped his share for a honey cake.

"I had no choice," he moaned. "My innards were emptier than a Dorian schoolroom. What else could I do?"

WORMS

Dan's tale has opened a can of colonial worms. Over the past few centuries thousands of Greeks have left the mainland for futures in countries all around the Mediterranean and Black Sea (see map for details).

The official line is that they're cultural ambassadors who are bringing Greek civilization and trade to places as far apart as Marseilles and Sebastopol.

BIG SNAG

But there are two big snags. **Not all the colonists want to go,** and when they get where they're going, **not everybody wants to see them there.**

"It's a real case of Don't Look Now," said an anxious Italian. "One minute you're lord and master of all you behold, the next there's a bunch of Greeks building towns and temples everywhere. We find it very upsetting that a load of total strangers should settle here without so much as a by-your-leave.

"They're mostly in the south, in places like Sicily. But if they could move even farther south we'd be very grateful. Better still, why don't they go home?"

However, the fact is that many colonists would like to do exactly that.

TOUGH

"I only left Corinth because there was no food," said Dan Delion. "I'd love to go back. But most of my shipmates can't. They're exiles, criminals and unemployed citizens. And anyway it's so far to row."

Back in Greece, the city-states are taking a tough line. "Come back? What nonsense!" said a Corinth spokesman. "These people are thieves and revolutionaries. All they do is eat our food which is in short enough supply as it is!

"And as for Mr. Delion's poverty. That's rich! We've had reports that in the Italian colony of Sybaris they sleep on rose petals and have banned roosters in case they wake them in the morning. Pah! **How soft can you get?"**

621 BC

There's no messing with tough-man Draco. The hard-hitting lawmaker from Athens has made it clear that he supports the maximum penalty for criminal activities – death.

"It's very worrying," said one Athenian thief. "We voted the man in because we'd had enough of tyrants and thought we needed a few laws. But we didn't count on this. **It's positively draconian."**

BAG

Under the new regime you can be executed for the smallest transgression. Steal a bag of olives and you're for the high jump. Extreme? Not a bit. When we spoke to Draco himself he explained the situation.

"Crime's a problem in Athens like any other big city," he said. "It may seem unfair that thieves and murderers are treated alike. But a crime's a crime isn't it? Death is the obvious answer. I'm only sorry that we haven't come up with something nastier for the really bad offenders. Still. There's time yet."

A Greek worrying about what "Wacko" Draco will do next.

SPARTA TALKS TOUGH

PRIVATES ON PARADE

613 BC

The Spartans are seething. After 17 years of defeats and internal rebellions they've decided to get their act together.

"It's a simple matter," said one Spartan colonel. "Ever since the Dark Ages we've been the top dogs in this part of the country. But recently we've let things slide. From now on, every Spartan man is going to have to learn to be a soldier."

So, it's goodbye to sleeping late on Sunday. Instead, it's cold baths at dawn and marches at midnight for the brave boys in the barracks. And everybody has to go naked.

"We're rather astonished," said a Theban citizen. "Being good at fighting's one thing, but this is totally unreasonable. **The Spartans spend their whole time preparing for war**. Even the women have to stay fit so that they can have healthy warrior babies.

"While the men are in barracks their wives spend their time doing athletics. And they wear very short tunics or sometimes nothing at all! You can imagine how distracting that is.

"But then Sparta's always been a little odd. It doesn't allow foreigners into the country. It's got two kings. And as for its political system – well, let's just say nobody can make head nor tail of it."

Sparta has run up against one or two problems in its army-mania. The main one is that with all the men in barracks, there's nobody to look after the farms.

They got around this by making the local peasants do the farming. But the peasants dislike it so much that the Spartans have to spend their whole time putting down rebel-lions, leaving them with no time to fight their enemies.

"I've come up with a fantastic answer to this problem," one Spartan general told the *Gazette*. "We need to persuade other states to form the **Peloponnesian League**. We'll demand that everyone in southern Greece gives Sparta military assistance when it's needed."

A Spartan soldier. No doing the dusting, cooking the supper and looking after the children for this fellow!

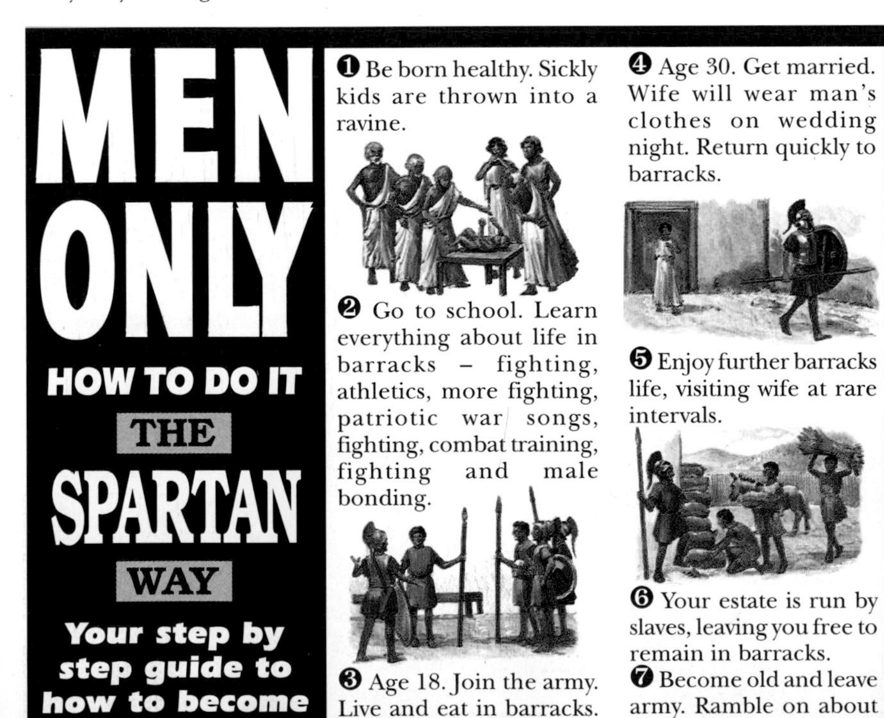

MEN ONLY

HOW TO DO IT THE SPARTAN WAY

Your step by step guide to how to become a tough nut

❶ Be born healthy. Sickly kids are thrown into a ravine.

❷ Go to school. Learn everything about life in barracks – fighting, athletics, more fighting, patriotic war songs, fighting, combat training, fighting and male bonding.

❸ Age 18. Join the army. Live and eat in barracks. Enjoy harsh conditions.

❹ Age 30. Get married. Wife will wear man's clothes on wedding night. Return quickly to barracks.

❺ Enjoy further barracks life, visiting wife at rare intervals.

❻ Your estate is run by slaves, leaving you free to remain in barracks.

❼ Become old and leave army. Ramble on about the joys of barracks life.

THE PRICE IS RIGHT!

500 BC

What on earth is this???

That's the question being asked by shopkeepers throughout Greece. Well, the *Gazette*'s got the answer. It's a **coin**. Or, as our finance editor calls it, "A small, round piece of metal you can buy things with."

The great advantage of coins is that they're so handy. Before, everyone used to barter. This meant that if you wanted to sell a cow you'd have to exchange it for, say, a table, some pots, a load of firewood and maybe a stool or two. And if you wanted to buy some meat or eggs you'd have to go into town with a fish and a bag of carrots. Imagine dragging all that around with you! Now you can just saunter along with some money.

Money. That's what I want.

Coins were invented in the Turkish state of Lydia, and they've quickly caught on over here. They're made of gold, silver or electrum (a mixture of both)and have pictures on both sides so you can tell if someone's tried to chip pieces off.

They're so popular that every state is minting its own except Sparta.

"We're not having any of this namby-pamby stuff," said the Spartan Banker-General. "We use iron bars for currency. If anyone tries to overcharge, you simply open your wallet, take out a bar and whack him on the head. You couldn't do that with a coin could you?"

No you couldn't!

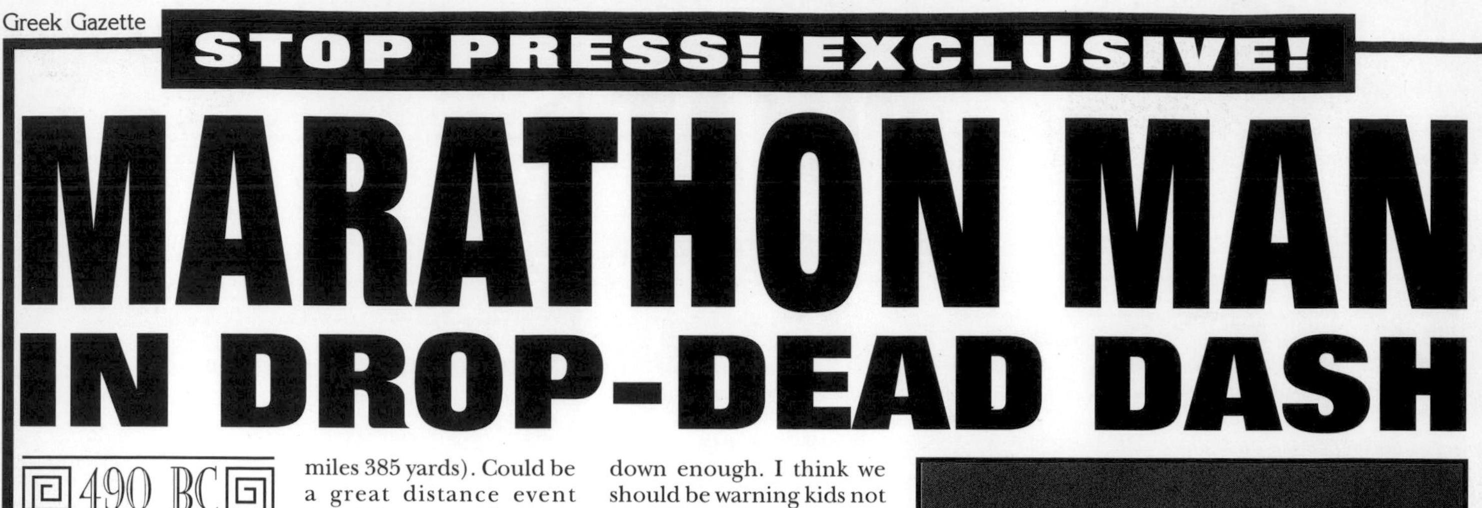

490 BC

Only a few hours ago top long-distance runner Phidippides staggered into Athens.

"I've just come from Marathon," he panted. "We've one..."

Then he dropped dead before he could finish his sentence. Citizens are scratching their heads. What was he trying to say? Luckily our sports correspondent, Vizzy Goth, can explain the mystery.

"It's quite simple. Phid was a dead serious athlete, always on the lookout for new races to win. He spotted the distance between Marathon and Athens and thought, "Hmmm! 42.195 km (25 miles 385 yards). Could be a great distance event here." So he gave it a try.

What he was trying to say before he died was, "We've one more race to compete in!"

HIGHLY UNLIKELY

"Yes, Viz," says our medical expert, "Doc" Epidaurus, "You're quite right. But you've left out an important detail. Before this epic event Phid had tried something even more ambitious. He'd run non-stop from Marathon to Sparta to warn them that the Persians were invading.

At several hundred miles this was clearly too far for competition purposes. And I think his death was a direct result of trying the Marathon-Athens dash when he hadn't warmed down enough. I think we should be warning kids not to try this at home."

"Too true Doc," says Vizzy Goth! "But even if they can't do it at home I'd like kids to know that the Marathon is now a competable distance!" **Remember! You read it first in the GAZETTE!!!**

489 BC

It has been drawn to the Gazette's attention that the story concerning Phidippides contains an error. His last words were in fact, "We've won!" referring to the epic battle at Marathon in which Athenian hoplites thrashed a Persian army twice their size, killing 6,400 of the enemy while sustaining only 192 casualties themselves, thereby boosting morale to such an extent that the battle would be remembered as an example of Athenian pluck and tenacity and as a reason why Athens should be the leading state in Greece. The Gazette apologizes for this inaccuracy.

"I like to sing as I go," Phidippides told the *Gazette* during his run. *"I get around, You better run, Run-run-runaway,* that sort of thing."

The *Gazette* war artist depicts the bridge across the Hellespont. Watch out, there's a storm coming!!

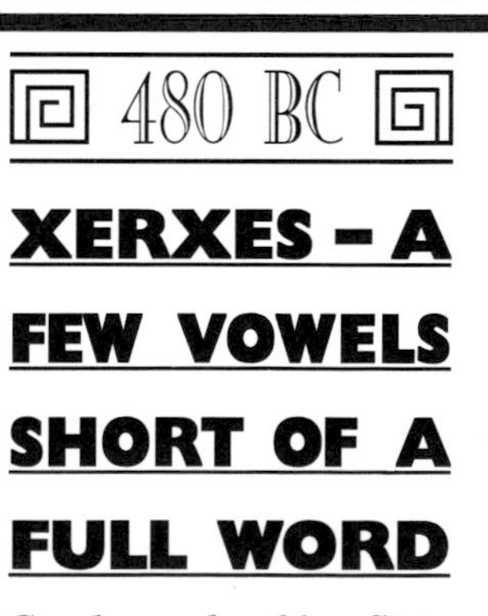

Greeks are laughing fit to burst as news comes in of the latest Persian fiasco. Having gathered the biggest invasion force in world history, King "Silly" Xerxes decided to invade Greece. But "Silly" went off the rails when he tried to cross the Hellespont, the strip of water dividing Greece from Turkey. He built a bridge by lashing together 300 boats and was all set to march across when a storm blew up and sent his bridge to the bottom.

"Silly" was so annoyed that he had the Hellespont punished.

- **He gave it 300 lashes.**
- **Then he branded it with hot irons.**
- **Then he chained it by throwing a lot of shackles into the water.**
- **And then, just to show it how lightly it had got off, he beheaded all the bridge-builders.**

What a laugh!

The *Gazette* says, **"Play it again Xerx!"**

OH DEAR, WHAT CAN "THERM" MATTER BE?

Our war artist depicts the battle of Thermopylae. "What I really like to draw is kittens," he complained.

PERSIANS CRUSH GREEKS IN MULTIPLE VICTORY SHOCK

480 BC

Greece was recovering yesterday from a bad dose of the Persian Blues. At the battle of Thermopylae King Xerxes's cool cats annihilated a Spartan army led by King Leonidas.

"It was a close-run thing," claimed Leonidas's next-of-kin. "There were only 7,000 of our men against the entire Persian army. We beat back three separate attacks until a traitor showed Xerxes how to get behind our positions. Our Leo ordered everyone to retreat, then stayed behind with 300 men and fought to the death."

It turns out King Xerxes isn't such a sad sack after all. After his first failure he built a second bridge over the Hellespont and trampled Greece into the ground. **Not only has he beaten the Spartans at Thermopylae but he's gone on to sack Athens**.

"Ha! Tremble puny Greeklings!" said the Persian monarch in a *Gazette* exclusive interview. "From now on you'll have to call me King 'Conqueror' Xerxes."

The secret behind the Persian success is a 10,000-strong band of elite soldiers called The Immortals. They do exactly what the king tells them and they're called immortal because as soon as one is killed another steps forward to take his place.

"This isn't the Greek way," said one Athenian officer. "Sparta's an exception of course. But generally we like to do things in a more democratic fashion. Like we did at Marathon, where we had a rota of ten generals alternating on a daily basis, with everyone voting what to do on each day. Come to think of it, it's a miracle we won.

"I'm not sure what the current consensus is. But if we can't beat the Persians on land I'm sure our navy can at sea."

STOP PRESS

479 BC

THREE-TIME WINNERS DITCH PERSIANS

At the battles of **Salamis** and **Mykale** a joint city-states navy has sent the Persians packing! Despite being outnumbered, our gallant boys rammed the Persian boats repeatedly with their trireme warships until every last one was at the bottom of the sea. At the same time a big bunch of hoplites annihilated The Immortals at **Plataea**. HA HA HA!!!

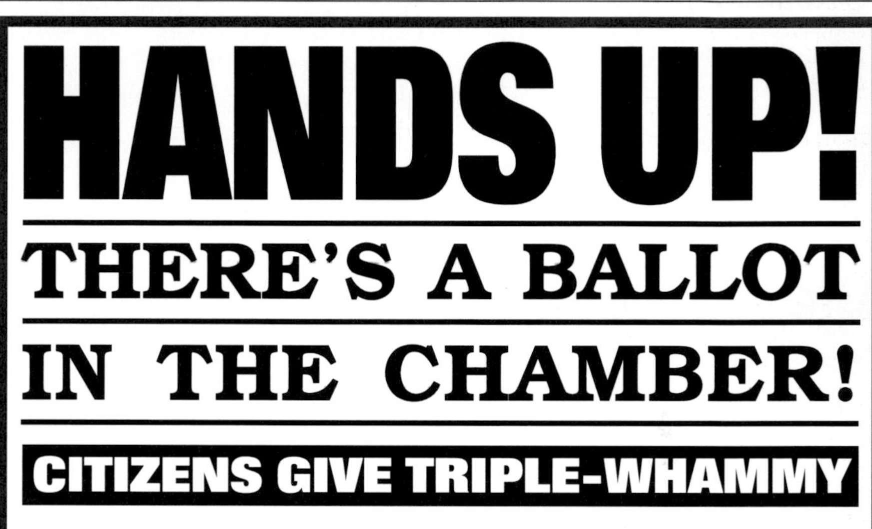

HANDS UP!

THERE'S A BALLOT IN THE CHAMBER!

CITIZENS GIVE TRIPLE-WHAMMY

461 BC

Athenian aristocrats are reeling as citizens give them the triple-whammy.

The **first blow** came in 594 BC when Solon introduced reforms to improve the lives of poorer people.

The **second smash** came in 508 when Cleisthenes announced that all citizens were equal.

The **knock-out clincher** came this year when Athenians rose up and seized all power for themselves. Pundits have already given the new system of government a name – **democracy**.

MOOD

Pericles, one of Athens's elected leaders, was in an expansive mood when he spoke to a *Gazette* reporter.

"What happened was that the earlier reforms weren't working as they should. Sure, we had an assembly and limited voting powers. But the city was still being run by a council of aristocrats called the Areopagus. Imagine our shame – being governed by something that sounds like an internal organ! There was only one solution: an armed uprising.

"We waited until our ruler had gone off with 4,000 hoplites to help Sparta put down a rebellion. Then we struck. It was all over in a matter of hours.

"Aristocratic rule is dead. From now on everything will be decided by a show of hands."

DOWN

Democracy has gone down well. Every citizen has an equal say, and all over Athens people are busy thinking up new things to vote on.

"I've just come back from a meeting," panted Aristotle Megaphon, a baker. "We came to all sorts of decisions – to break off relations with Sparta, to get ready for war, to appoint some generals and to build up the navy. **Isn't democracy fantastic?**"

FOR FULL DETAILS SEE OUR DEMOCRACY SPECIAL ON PAGES 28-29.

Pericles. Crazy hat, but not so crazy political idea!

PERSIANS ON THE CARPET

GAZETTE PAGE 10 COMMENT

A Persian. This man might look funny, but that doesn't mean he won't burn your house and steal your chariot.

448 BC

12 GOOD REASONS why we don't like Persians

Let's face it. Everybody loathes them. And here's why. They're a load of bullies who've taken over the Middle East, over-run the Egyptians, invaded us twice and given us no end of grief with their funny beards and so-called Immortals. Just look at what they've done.

- **Started from nothing in a particularly barren part of Iran.**
- **Took over next-door Media 550 BC.**
- **Seized Turkey 547 BC.**
- **Grabbed Palestine and Babylonia 539 BC.**
- **Occupied Egypt 525 BC.**
- **Moved into India 521 BC.**
- **But then...they invaded *us* in 490 BC and were totally TRASHED at Marathon.**
- **However...they invaded us again in 480 BC and *we* were wiped out at Thermopylae.**
- **Then they went on to sack Athens the same year.**
- **But *we* sent them packing at Salamis, Mykale and Plataea in 480 and 479 BC.**
- **Made a peace treaty with us in 449 BC.**
- **But they're still skulking about trying to have another go at us. Typically OUTRAGEOUS!**

The Gazette says "Go home you feared and disliked people whom our oracles predict will eventually be conquered by the Greeks, peace treaty or no peace treaty."

That's telling them!

AN OFFICIAL ANNOUNCEMENT PLACED BY THE CITY-STATE OF ATHENS

YOU THERE!

Yes you, you weak little Aegean states who've hardly got two warships to rub together

- Frightened of another Persian invasion?
- Do you know what Persians do when they're really angry?
- Did you know that after their recent defeat the Persians are **really, really** angry?
- Are you shaking in your sandals?

Good. Now pay attention.
Because we're inviting you to join the Delian League.

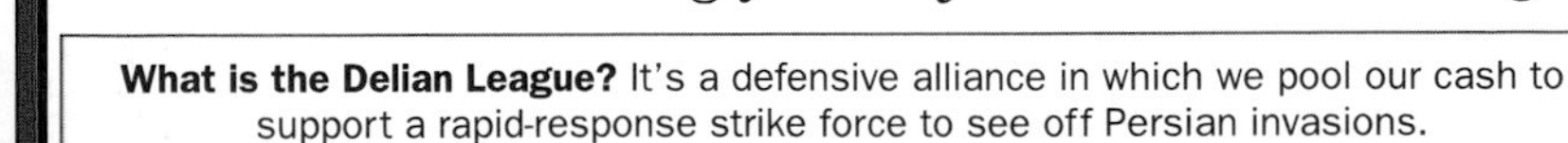

What is the Delian League? It's a defensive alliance in which we pool our cash to support a rapid-response strike force to see off Persian invasions.

What does it mean for you? Very little. All you have to do is put your gold in a central fund on the island of Delos and do what we tell you.

What does it mean for us? We keep our fleet of 200 warships on constant alert ready to defend you against the vile Persians.

What could be better? Apply in writing while you still can.

Under the terms of the Delian League in the year 478 BC the state of Athens recognizes that there will be no Persian invasion and reserves the future right to spend all League gold to its own benefit – i.e on sprucing up the city, developing the economy, importing fancy goods, building the Parthenon, etc. – and the right thereby to call the 440s and thereafter the Athenian Golden Age, and the right to conquer any member states that may or may not put up a fuss and ultimately the right thereby to create an empire that stretches across the Aegean.

SYSTEME VGOOD

Sunlight becomes you, it goes with your hair... Or does it?

*Is your hair crisp and dry? Then take a look at the label on your shampoo urn. If it doesn't say **Virgin Greek Olive Oil Dealers** you've got the answer. Nobody pampers your coiffure like VGOOD. We want your locks to look shinier than the seat of a philosopher's tunic. **So get hip, get VGOOD.***

SMELL SWELL

with Penelope's Perfumes.

Ladies! Unlock the secrets of social success with one of our quality lotions. Try the ever-popular Scent of the Gods, made from cedar oil, honey, salt, myrrh and balsam.

Penelope's Perfumes.

Available in fashionable foot-style bottles.

WEAPONS SPECIAL WEAPONS SPECIAL WEAPONS SPECIAL

TRI-MENDOUS!!

The Gazette guide to the super ship they're calling the Trireme

OARSMEN

Each seat comes complete with lacy cushion, waitress service and personal video screen. (Just kidding!)

Now hear this! They say bad things come in threes, and if you're a Persian or a Phoenician they don't come badder than Greece's new navy blockbuster THE TRIREME.

- **three times the speed**
- **three times the control**
- **three times the ramming power**

All thanks to new three level oar technology!

Once upon a time warships just carried troops who landed on shore to fight their battles. Then some bright spark found out you could actually fight at sea – ship to ship.

RAM

More recently naval tacticians have discovered that the most cost-effective, tough-on-them-and-soft-on-us technique is to ram the enemy to sink his ship. It's much less messy than hand-to-hand fighting. And much more fun too!

But ramming needs speed and control, and there's no better way to achieve that than **more oars**. So navy designers have hit on the idea of stacking the oarsmen three levels high along each side of the ship. The result – **the most powerful weapon this side of Zeus's thunderbolts!!**

CARP

However, the super ship does have its critics. There's no space to cook or sleep so the trireme can only operate within reach of a friendly port or beach. 24-hour blockades are also out of the question as the ship has to return to shore every night. But let's not quibble. The *Gazette* says "With boats like these Greece can RULE THE WAVES!!!!"

CHECK OUT THESE FEATURES....

❶ Three banks of oarsmen whisk you along at speeds of up to 16kmph. (10mph).
❷ Crew of 200 salty sea dogs, including archers and hoplites to repel enemy boarders.
❸ Mast made from finest Macedonian spruce. Can be lowered for battle.
❹ Sail of toughest linen. Stow this away for ultimate control! (Stripes optional.)
❺ Bronze ram for those close encounters of the Aegean kind.
❻ Reinforced prow with big painted eye to frighten the opposition. Oooo!
❼ Upper-deck archers' nest. Aieee!
❽ Oars. Each a massive 4m (14ft). Wow!
❾ Leather rowlock covers. No water gets in when these are in place!
❿ Experienced captain from a top-locker aristocratic family. Aye aye, Sir!

NEXT WEEK: LONG SPEARS – ARE THEY WORTH THE EFFORT?

IT'S A PELOPO-KNEES-UP!

404 BC

Sparta's hard guys are whooping it up tonight. Why? Because the Peloponnesian War is over. After a hard 30 years struggle between Athens and Sparta, Sparta has finally WON!

"It took almost three decades but we got there in the end," explained Spartan general Lysander to our war correspondent. "Despite a number of setbacks we hammered them fair and square.

"The reason it took so long was because we had the best army in Greece but Athens had the best navy. Whenever we tried to besiege them they just brought in food by sea. Stalemate!

"Then we had this fantastic brainwave. We built a navy too! We followed the Athenians to a place called Aegospotami and waited until they'd all gone ashore for a picnic. After that it was easy. We captured 170 of their ships and executed 4,000 prisoners.

"The next year they surrendered. We pulled down their walls, got rid of their stupid democracy and installed not one but THIRTY tyrants to run the place.

"What a hoot! Have some more bread and water."

"What are *you* looking at?" A Spartan behaving badly.

KING PHIL'S MACEDONIAN MASH-UP

BOONDOCK BOYS HIT BIG TIME

338 BC

Whoops! Maybe those city-states aren't so hot after all. Athens and Thebes have just been smashed at the battle of Chaeronea by a bunch of bumpkin northerners called the Macedonians.

"We're gutted," said an Athenian spokesman. "We'd always thought the Macedonians were useless. They speak such bad Greek you can only just understand them. In fact, we're not really sure they ARE Greeks. Until 20 years ago they hardly had an army because so many of them had been killed in civil wars. I don't know how they suddenly got so powerful. **It's probably something to do with that King Phil.**"

Philip II, as he prefers to be called, revealed all to the *Gazette*.

"When I came to the throne in 360 BC, Macedonia was a mess. But I soon put things in order. I built up the army and conquered all the locals to make an empire three times as big as all the southern city-states put together. After this latest victory I'm sure the Peloponnesians will recognize who's boss. **And my name's not Phil it's Philip.**"

Phil's bright ideas include giving his hoplites gigantic spears so they can walk the enemy off the field without even having to get near them. He's also invented two elite units – the Companion Cavalry and Companion Infantry – for hand-to-hand fighting.

The spears and Companions are a clear winner. And soothsayers predict this is only the start.

Mystic Mag of Megara says: "Using the latest divination methods, I have observed the flight of birds and recorded the last few lightning strikes. The portents suggest Greece will unite to fight the Persians. The Greeks will call themselves the *Hellenes* and create one of the **biggest empires ever**.

"Yet wait! What do I see in my magic mirror? The leader of this empire will not be Philip. It will be another. The words are hard to make out but... yes, it is one called **Rednaxela**!"

King Phil – Macedonia's man of the moment.

YOUR GUIDE TO KING PHIL'S TOPPEST TROOPS

THERE'S NOTHING LIKE A PAL!

"Posh and pugnacious?" ask King Philip and his son Alexander, "then join The Companions!"

Phil and Alex are seeking fit young men of noble stock to join their close-knit team of elite battle executives. If you are a thrusting, get-ahead infantryman with a persuasive fighting manner then you're just the man for the job.

If you become a Companion you'll travel the known world, and be in with a big chance to **annihilate** Asia Minor*, **pillage** Palestine, petrify Persia, **intimidate** India and **exterminate** Egypt! **What more could a rough-and-tumble, jabbing-and-stabbing kind of a guy ask for!**

*That's Turkey, geography fans!

A Companion contemplating combat with the Persians.

GORDIANS IN KNOT FIASCO

"MONEY FOR OLD ROPE," SAYS HUNKY NEW KING

333 BC

It's Empire Time folks! He's been fighting the Persians for only a year, but already Macedonia's King Alexander looks set to become Asia's next No. 1.

The vibrant young king showed his style at the town of Gordium in Turkey today when he solved their famous wagon-and-pole puzzle. The knot which joined the wagon to the pole was so complicated that an oracle declared that **whoever untangled it would become Lord of all Asia**.

His brainy Majesty, who studied under Aristotle, one of the greatest philosophers of all time, gave the knot the benefit of his education. **He took out his sword and cut it in half**.

"This is divine proof that I am going to wipe those Persian scum from the face of the earth," crowed Alex to cries of "Cheat!" from the crowd.

But if Alexander's happy the Gordians aren't. "It's a great blow to the tourist industry," said a town spokesman. "Our knot was all we had. What'll we do now? I suppose we'll have to highlight one of our other features. But between you and me the **Gordian Dusty Market Place** doesn't have quite the same ring as the **Gordian Knot**."

Alexander. "To be or knot to be," he quipped before slicing.

STOP PRESS...

The oracle was right!!! Reports are reaching the *Gazette* that Alexander's army have just smashed King Darius's troops at the Battle of Issus!!!

Mired down by enemies? Not if you fit our "Darius Demons" to your chariot. Based on an original model used by King Darius of Persia, these super-sharp, long-lasting axle blades are at the cutting edge of technology. They'll make mincemeat of any opposition. Simply snap 'em on and let your chariot do the work. The faster you go the more mayhem you'll create! You'll cut a dash on any battlefield - GUARANTEED!

Can be used in peacetime too! With a pair of "Darius Demons" it's GOODBYE to parking problems and inner-city congestion. People lining the street? No hassle! You pull in, they pull out - and if they don't they'll wish they had!

The Freeway, Alexandria.
"The One-Stop Shop For All Your Charioteering Requirements."

WARNING: Despite their potential for thrills, particularly when cornering, "Darius Demons" have not been approved for speed testing or competitive use. Regretfully we must advise racing owners not to attach this equipment to stadium chariots.

IMPORTANT! Battle performance can be adversely affected if the enemy simply parts ranks and pelts you with stones as you drive through. In such situations Chariots of Fire Products takes no responsibility for any adverse outcome.

LION MAN BUILDS CITY

A PHAROS DAY'S PAY FOR A PHAROS DAY'S WORK

Thrusting young architect Dinocrates finally got the break he wanted. Having trailed Alexander's army all over Persia he got miffed at the way nobody took any notice of him. So he dressed up in a lion skin and walked around carrying a big club. They noticed him then!

"This is the kind of get-ahead attitude I like to see," Alexander told him. "Build me a new capital for Egypt. Put it here, just where the Nile stops and the sea starts. Let's really push the boat out, youngster. No expense spared. I want people to be talking about this city for centuries."

"It was a hard commission," said jubilant Dino. "But I got it under control. I laid the city out on a grid plan, gave it an agora, a tree-lined park and a big double quay. But what it still needs is a lighthouse. Nobody's ever thought of that before! The city council is currently considering ideas.

"The only problem with the city was the name. The boss said it should be called Alexandria. Well, there are at least 15 other Alexandrias dotted around the Middle East by now, and most of them are grungy little villages. I thought since this was something special we could call it something different – like Dinocrates City, or Dino-on-sea, or Dinor Regis. But he put his foot down. And you don't argue with a foot that's conquered half the known world, do you? No sir!

"Still, beats going around in a lion skin for a living."

According to the *Gazette*'s oracle, Alexandria has a big future. She says,

"I predict it will be a hub of Greek civilization with the most famous library in the world, a population of at least half a million and a building called The Museum which will be a magnet for Greek scientists."

A wonder in the making? Architect sketch for the Pharos lighthouse, soon to be built in Alexandria.

NO MORE WAR! LAHORE'S A BORE

325 BC

It's all over! After ten years of successful campaigning Alexander's men have told him "We want to go home now!"

The surprise announcement followed a wipe-out victory in India, when Alex's army thrashed the King of Lahore and sent his 200 war elephants packing. But this time the troops weren't satisfied with victory. After another week's march into India they refused to go any further.

"We don't like Lahore and we're fed up with fighting," said an army rep. "We think we've done far too much already. In the last ten years we've...

- **walloped the Persians.**
- **occupied Palestine.**
- **grabbed Egypt.**
- **walked over Afghanistan.**
- **trampled the Indians into the ground.**
- **created the biggest empire the world has ever seen.**
- **shown everyone who's boss.**
- **left squiggly lines all over the map of Asia.**

Isn't that enough? *We* think it is."

RELUCTANT

Alexander has given in reluctantly to his troops' demands. Or at least he says he's reluctant. We think he's secretly relieved. Not only has he married the beautiful Roxane, daughter of an Afghan chieftain, but camp gossip says he plans to marry a second wife when he gets to Persia.

AMOROUS

Our social correspondent writes: "Alexander obviously has his mind on other things. There is no doubt that a long campaign puts a man in an amorous mood. He and Roxane face a long journey through hot deserts.

"But once he's cooled down Alex will want to get into the Persian swing, and what better way to do that than marry a Persian wife? Nothing odd in that, particularly if you're an emperor.

DRAINS

"But I'd advise his wives to watch him vigilantly. They should be particularly careful not to let him inspect a Babylonian drainage project in 323 BC. The portents suggest he will be bitten by an infected mosquito and die a few days later. And after that things will really go down hill."

WHERE DID YOU GET THAT HAT, SIR?

Even if you haven't campaigned with Alexander in Persia you can still look your fellow citizens in the eye with our quality "doff 'n don" Phrygian helmets. As issued to all self-respecting veterans. Don it for that martial air! Doff it for the lenient conqueror look!

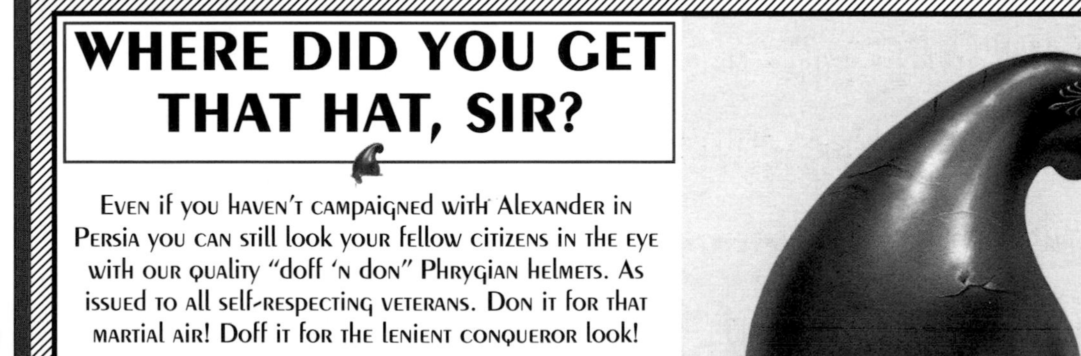

One size fits all.
Specify blue-painted for enlisted men or feather-plumed for officers.

Phrygian Products, Persepolis, Persia

(Due to severe sacking and razing-to-the-ground by Greek armies we are unable to supply a full street address. Please direct your messenger to "the only house with three walls left standing." Thank you.)

QUADRUPLE ROYAL MURDER SENSATION

301 BC

"Not us," say benefactors as Alexander's empire collapses

In the 22 years since Alexander's death, his generals have divided his empire among themselves, and his court has become a foaming, swirling whirlpool of blind ambition, deadly intrigue and even deadlier murder. His mother Olympias, wife Roxane, son Alexander and half-brother Philip Arrideus have all died in mysterious circumstances – almost certainly killed. His main general is also dead. The once great Alexandrian Empire has fractured into three rival factions.

Nobody knows who committed the ghastly crimes. But three men are sitting pretty at the head of each faction as a result. We interviewed them on your behalf.

THE PRIME SUSPECTS

1. Mr. Ptolemy of Egypt.

"I was nowhere near anywhere where the murders occurred. I was having a nice glass of wine with my friends in Alexandria on all possible occasions. When the news came through I was shocked. Send my condolences to the relatives and tell them I've taken the precaution of making myself Pharaoh of Egypt."

2. Mr. Antigonas of Greece.

"Isn't it awful? And all of them within such a short space of time! I was just a small child at the time of the murders, so it wasn't anything to do with me. But if it's any consolation I'd like to announce that I plan to take over Greece in 276 BC, and control the country by keeping garrisons in all major cities."

3. Mr. Seleucus of All-The-Rest.

"Those two have got it easy. They're running self-contained countries. Me? I've got to handle an empire stretching from Palestine to India. It'll break up at any minute! And they're going on about condolences? Get a life! Sorry I didn't send any flowers. Alex was a great guy. OK? End of interview. **I'm busy**."

Our political correspondent writes: "I'm afraid the end is nigh. Whoever did the dirty deed, it's obvious that Alexander's empire is on its last legs. It's only a matter of time before everything falls to pieces. I'd give Greece about 150 years then it'll all be over."

ONE FOR THE WOAD

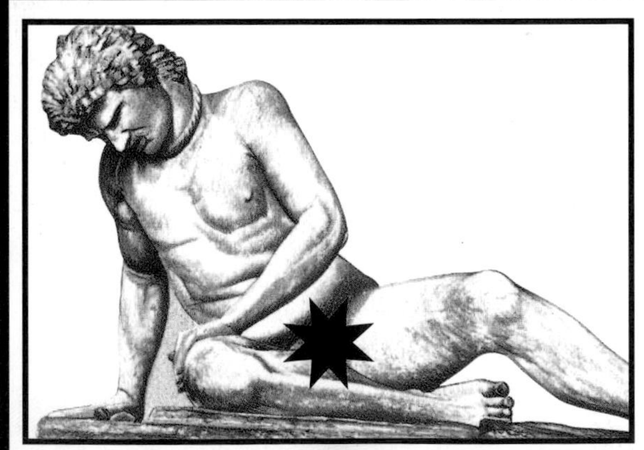

A dying Celt. He's blue really, but the *Gazette*'s resident sculptor told us: "I'm not ruining a perfectly good piece of marble with blue paint. Be off with you!"

297 BC

Celts give last orders in Greece

Invading Celts have decided to get out of Greece after enduring a horror-packed night of fear.

The woady wuffians – trademark: spiky yellow hair and a blue skin dye called woad – have rampaged throughout northern Greece. But they withdrew from an all-out assault on Delphi following a **stunning series of natural disasters**.

General Brennus of Gaul, the Celtic leader, was angry at the way things turned out.

"First we had an earthquake. Then there was lightning and thunder followed by a fierce storm. Then there was a night of frost and snow. And in the morning we were hit by rockfalls.

"We like a fight as much as the next man but this just isn't fair. We're going to leave Greece and set up a small colony in Turkey instead."

Reports say that the Celts were so afraid of the weather that they jumped up and tried to kill it with their swords. Result: a lot of wounded Celts.

The *Gazette* is worried. If a load of heavy-drinking barbarians can get this far, who's next? **There's lots of them out there and they all want a slice of our civilization. Be on guard, citizens!**

IT'S CURTAINS FOR CORINTH

CITY CRUSHED IN ROMAN RAMPAGE

These coarse little men are Romans. Ugh!

146 BC

"Vulgar" newcomers set the agenda

Wow! What an extremely unpleasant surprise! The Romans have burned Corinth to the ground and crushed Greek independence.

"No one will live in this city for 100 years," bragged Roman consul Lucius Mummius as he strode through the smoking ruins of Corinth followed by thousands of crack Roman legionaries and a convoy of siege weapons stretching to the horizon.

"This is fighting talk!" said an Athenian onlooker. "But we'll let it pass for now."

SNEAKS

The Romans have been sneakily conquering Greek territory for some time. First it was the colonies, then it was parts of western Greece, then it was Macedonia. Now it's the city-state heartland – the Peloponnese.

"What they do," explained a singed Corinthian, "is conquer next door and tell you that you can remain free so long as you behave yourself. Then if you do the slightest thing wrong they're on top of you like a ton of coals."

The Romans have taken everyone by surprise. Until recently they were a bunch of nobodies with a low-grade democratic political system. Now they run the whole Mediterranean. What's more, they've stolen Greek architecture and Greek gods and are trying to pass them off as their own.

FRIGHT

"We are well acquainted with Romans," said Lady Helen of Thebes. "They often come to visit and are very polite and respectful, with a lot of cash to flash around. You can tell they admire us. They shower the oracles with gold. And they're building temples just like ours, back in Rome. **But between you and me, they're frightfully vulgar!**"

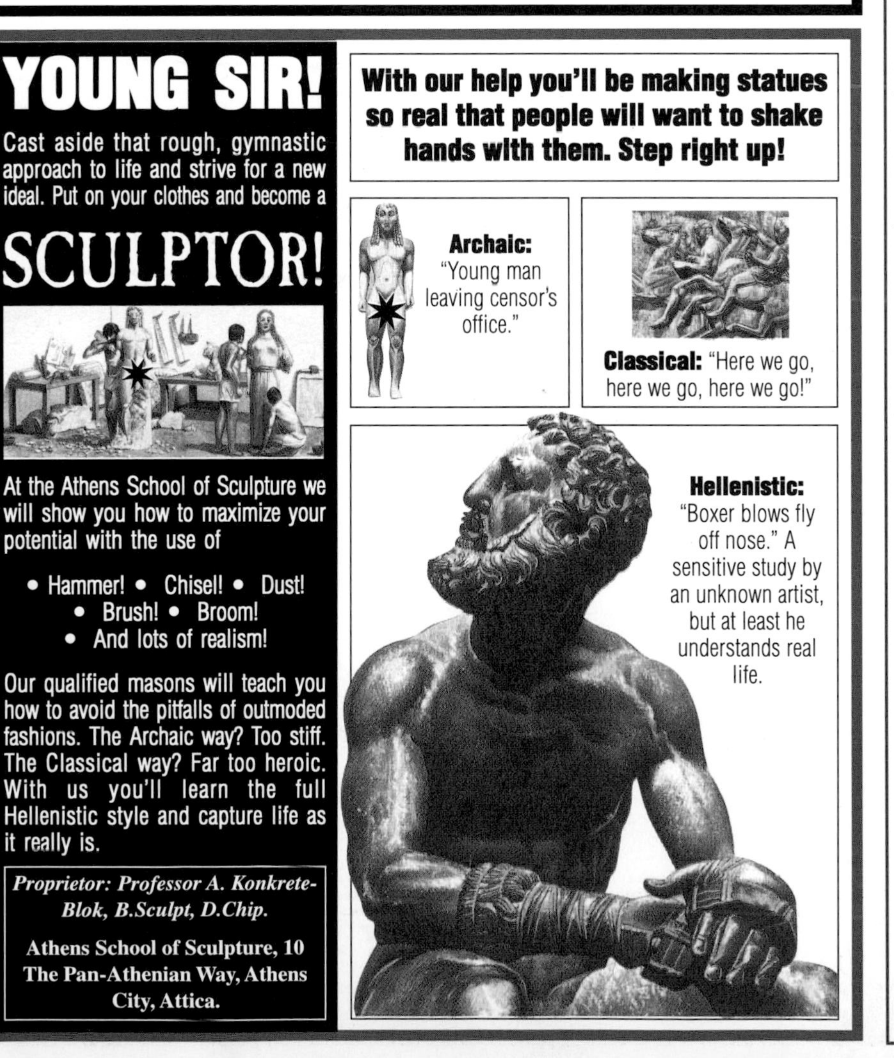

Another era's over and what a busy one it's been!

What a time we've had, eh? We've invented geometry, city-states, and democracy. We've set up colonies all over the Mediterranean. We've crushed the Persians and created a massive empire.

STAMP

And if you read on you'll realize we've not only stamped our name on the cultural map, we've walked all over it! Drama, architecture, literature, the Olympic Games – you name it, we've started it! We bet people will be copying us up to the 20th century and beyond.

END

But all good things have to come to an end, and our vibrant world has passed into the hands of the Romans* who operate the most grabbing-est greediest, no-account civilization we've ever seen.

Isn't that a pity folks? Just when we were enjoying ourselves, too. But don't worry! No one's going to forget us, that's for sure!

* If you want to learn more about these vulgarians you might be interested in a sordid, sensationalist, down-market tabloid called "The Roman Record", masquerading as a quality newspaper in bookshops throughout the land.

ANOTHER UNIQUE OFFER FROM THE OLYMPIC MINT!
THE OLYMPIC MINT
is proud to present its latest collection
PLATTERS O' GODS.
There can be no doubt that, for appreciators of peerless pottery, our platters are the ultimate. Hand-tooled from the finest clay, these nine masterpieces depicting the major gods of Olympus will add class to any shelf in the land. Your house guests will carry away with them an indelible impression of grandeur.
PLATTERS O' GODS include all the best known Olympians. Sign up with us and, once a month for the next nine months, we will send you the following panoply of magnificence.
ZEUS
This top god just can't keep his hands off the ladies. But watch it, angry hubbies! He's handy with a thunderbolt.
HERA
Wife of Zeus – his sister too, oo-er. This long-suffering beauty looks after women and marriage.
APHRODITE
The luscious goddess of love. No one can resist her charms. Definitely one for adults only!
ARES
The brutal god of war is not a deity to meet in a dark alley. Aphrodite loves him though! Aren't women funny?
HESTIA
Goddess of the hearth. She's so ordinary she left Olympus to live with us mortals. And you can't get more ordinary than that.
PLUTO
The original man in black, he's the last god you want to meet. In fact, as King of the Underworld he IS the last god you'll meet.
APOLLO
The hardest working god in the business. Apollo starts at dawn and doesn't stop till dusk. Who is he? The sun god, of course!
HERMES
Paciest paper boy on the block, this Olympian wildster is the gods' messenger. Also looks after thieves and explorers.
What better way to start your collection than with – DIONYSUS.
The good-time god of wine, fertility and high-jinks is totally FREE and is yours as soon as you place your first order.
Apply within seven days and receive FREE a tasteful Mount Olympus paperweight. Our depiction of the home of the gods will add authority to even the most humble desk.
What some satisfied customers say about our products:
"My home has been transformed since I purchased your Great Tyrants plates. We have had more important people to visit than ever before." Mr. NB, Corinth.
"Your Wounds and Warfare series was a smash hit! Keep it up!" Colonel FYI, Sparta.
"Your Sandals Through The Centuries is one of the best buys I have ever made." Miss RSVP, Thebes.
"People look at me in a new light now that I own the full set of Loincloths Of Old." Ms DIY, Argos.
Send your orders to:
OLYMPIC MINT, 102 The Promenade, Chaeronea-upon-Thebes, Greece.

THE ORACLE SPEAKS

Live from Delphi, Madame Pythia is poised on her tripod to solve any query you put to her. In a mystic smog, produced by a brazier-full of aromatic herbs, the finest oracle in Greece offers uncanny insights into your personal problems. Love? Health? Family? Business? War? Plumbing? You ask it, she'll answer.

BAD OMEN

Q Dear Oracle, I went up to the Pnyx to have a debate – i.e. yell at all the speakers – when I felt a few drops of rain. To my astonishment everyone went home. They even left their barbecue behind. What's going on?

A *You silly citizen. Obviously this is your first time at an Assembly. Any fool knows that no debate can take place when it rains because rain is a bad omen. Besides which it makes people wet. And the so-called barbecue is in fact a burned sacrifice to the gods.*

JUST SUPPOSING

Q Dear Oracle, I am a Greek peasant. But supposing I wasn't, could you tell me the best time to invade Greece?

A *I divine that you are a Persian king and will therefore give you no answer save, "Don't even think of it!"*

LOW WATER TABLE

Q Dear Oracle, What is an Archimedes Screw? How can I get one? I am a 70-year-old farmer with a low water table who is constantly searching for new ways of getting it up.

A *You must be referring to the method of raising water through a tube from a lower level to a higher level, by means of an ingenious screw-like device, as invented by the scientist Archimedes.*

These can be obtained in most agoras for a few drachmas.

KEEN

Q Dear Oracle, I am a Spartan veteran who takes a keen interest in military holidays. Could you tell me when Greek armies are most commonly off duty and thus unable to repel invasions?

A *You are a transparent Persian king. But since your letter included several gold coins I can tell you that nobody does any fighting when they're bringing in the harvest.*

MISSING MRS.

Q Dear Oracle, I haven't been able to locate my wife for several weeks. Do you know where she is?

A *No probs. She's in the women's part of your house. You know, the gynaeceum, where all wives have to stay because they're not considered decent enough for everyday society. Why not knock on the door? See who's in there. You might also find a lot of daughters and nieces.*

BURNED

Q Dear Oracle, Isn't it lucky that our country doesn't have a tradition of pie-making? Imagine what would happen if Aristotle's wife said, "Your pie is in the oven." The poor man wouldn't know if it was a pie or the similarly sounding Pi, meaning the ratio of the circumference of a circle to its diameter, which he first calculated. Every mealtime he would fear his life's work had gone up in flames!

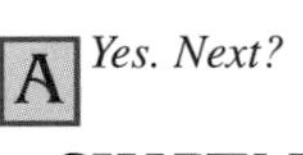

A *Yes. Next?*

SMARTY-PANTS

Q Dear Oracle, I am a young girl and I have so many toys I don't know what to do with them. I'm going to throw them away. This isn't a question. I just wanted to share this simple solution with you so you know you don't have to be a smarty-pants on a tripod to solve everyday problems.

A *Don't do it! Keep those toys intact! You'll need to sacrifice them to the goddess Artemis on your wedding day as a sign that your childhood is over. Great Colossus of Rhodes! I only hope it's not too late.*

NO KIDDING

Q Dear Oracle, Every night I walk along a remote path which is always lined with little babies. When I look in the morning they're gone. Are my friends playing a surreal trick on me? Or am I going mad?

A *You might well be going mad. More likely, you're walking along the path where poor people leave the kids they can't afford to bring up. Not to worry, though. These children will be removed by better-off families and trained as slaves. More important is your paranoia. Got any other problems? I can counsel privately too, you know.*

NOT YOU AGAIN

Q Dear Oracle, Where did I leave my sandals?

A *Under the bed as usual.*

PATTERNS

Q Dear Oracle, I am a student studying invasion patterns over the centuries. I'd like to pinpoint Greece's weakest areas. Can you tell me where they are?

A *Begone, you pernicious Persian fool.*

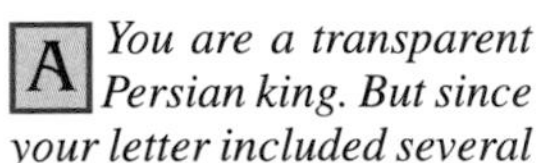

LETTER OF THE WEEK

Q Dear Oracle, I went to the gym because I was feeling flabby. To my horror it was full of men dancing about stark naked. I was so aghast I did not even bother to open my Adidos bag, and went straight home. Have any other readers had this problem?

A *You must be from out of town. Greek men are not renowned for their shyness. Particularly in the gym. In fact, the word "gymnos" means naked. So a "gymnasium" is a place you go in order to be naked. Get on down there and tone up those muscles!*

NO DILEMMA TOO THORNY! OUR GIRL IN THE GROTTO WILL PRONOUNCE ON ANYTHING!

PHILOSOPHY

It's philosophy week in the Gazette and we're marking the occasion with a double-page brain bonanza! What's life all about? Consult the Gazette guide to the Greeks with the greatest grey matter, and find out!

Gathered around for a serious think, Plato (left), fails to amuse his fellow philosophers when he pronounces "I'm pink therefore I'm spam".

WHICH PHILOSOPHER?

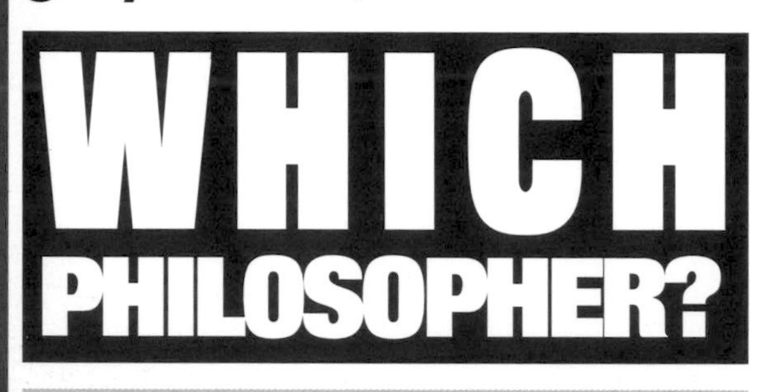

We took a consumer survey of eight great thinkers and asked our "schoolmaster" to award them marks.

He's given them between 1 to 3 brains for intelligence and 1 to 3 yawns for tedium. Aristotle came out tops with 3 brains but didn't make it into the best buy category because he also clocked up 2 yawns. We suggest you look for the mid-range thinkers who offer brain cells AND entertainment.

Thales

624-546 BC

The first philosopher ever! Said the world began as water. The original absent-minded professor – fell into a well while watching the stars. **Verdict**: a likely thale.

Anaximander

611-546 BC

Like Thales (but didn't fall down a well), and said men came from slime and were originally fish. **Verdict**: much more like it. Making good progress.

Pythagoras

580-500 BC

Bit of a weirdo. Ran a religious colony in Italy and didn't eat beans. Believed in the importance of numbers and revered triangles. Also believed in reincarnation and remembered all his previous lives. **Verdict**: takes all sorts. Good at numbers, but still hasn't learned to write.

Anaxagoras

500-428 BC

Another stargazer. Announced that the sun was a flaming mass, explained eclipses, and revealed the moon was a moon. Wrote a book about nature as a result. **Verdict:** innovative. But should spend less time looking out the window.

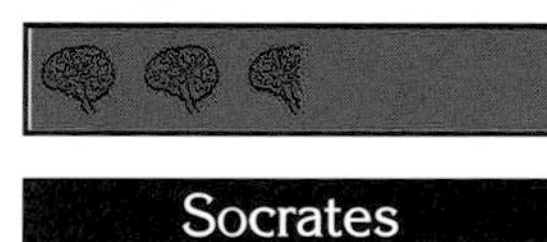

Socrates

470-399 BC

The man who stood still for days on end pondering life (when he wasn't partying!) Spent ages trying to work out how society should be run. His answer: everyone should be good. Ugliest man in Athens and too clever by half. **Verdict:** soc it to me. Excellent work.

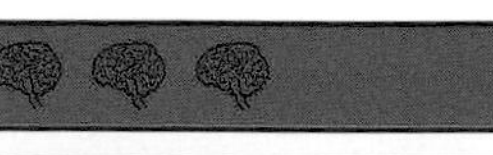

Plato

427-347 BC

Popular man, popular books. Thought Pythagoras was tops. Thought Socrates was even more tops. Founded Academy school in Athens and developed idea of perfect society based on virtue. **Verdict:** typical schoolmaster despot. A word after class, please.

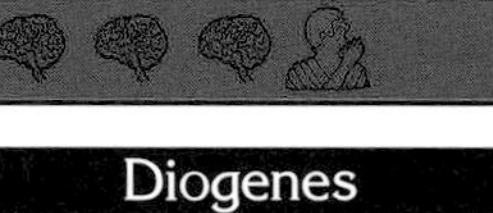

Diogenes

412-323 BC

Lived in a barrel and said everyone should have no possessions and live as close to nature as possible. Was picked on because he got on everyone's nerves. The original drop-out. **Verdict:** nothing in the lost-property cupboard. Good effort! (Bonus brain for entertainment.)

Aristotle

384-323 BC

Towering but impenetrable intellect. Told us all about nature, humans and Artemis-knows-what. Taught Alexander the Great. Invented logic. Here's a quote: "Man is mortal. Aristotle is a man. Aristotle is mortal." May look obvious but wasn't then. **Verdict:** Bright but dull! Definitely room for improvement.

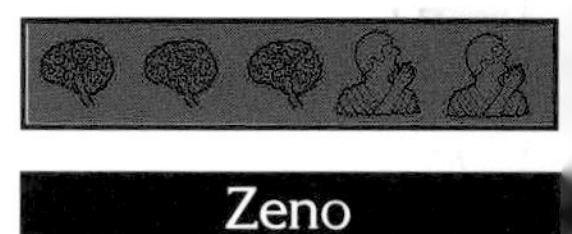

Zeno

336-264 BC

Nice, quiet, wine-and-pastries sort of guy. Said everyone should put up with the bad things that happen because that's life. **Verdict:** sloppy thinking. Well-meaning but must try harder. See me in my study.

Best Buy!

Plato. He's written more than any of the others. His ideas are a little dull but he's easy to understand.

Worth Considering

Socrates – because that's where Plato got his ideas from – and Diogenes because he's way ahead of his time. We would have chosen Aristotle but he's just too tedious.

WATCH

Here are some cuttings from our archives which just go to prove that brains and common sense aren't necessarily natural bed-fellows!!

399 BC Greek Gazette

CHOP SHOCK FOR SOC

"Hemlock? Make mine a double."

Party-loving philosopher Socrates was told to change his tipple yesterday when a trial jury ordered him to drink poison!

The shock sentence came after Athens's top egghead was accused of corrupting his students.

"It's a stitch-up!" said a pal. "All he said was that it was important to find the truth and to live by it because the soul was immortal. He was very big on right and wrong and didn't approve of corruption. The only thing he did was annoy the authorities by being too clever."

When the jury found him guilty they gave him a choice: go into exile or think up another suitable punishment. Soc suggested that he be maintained at public expense for the rest of his life. The court was so outraged they ordered him to take deadly hemlock.

"He's putting on a brave face," said his friend, "but he's obviously quite shaken. He feels they didn't give the matter enough thought. What it boils down to is that he'd made a lot of important people look stupid."

The *Gazette* says "Call that clever? Not in our scroll it isn't!"

360 BC Greek Gazette

D.PHIL V.DULL

SAY ATHENIANS

The brightest brain in town hit a flat note when he put forward his revolutionary theory – virtue is all.

Dr. Plato was greeted with massed yawns as he unveiled his new lifestyle plan. According to him, democracy should be abolished, Athens should be ruled by philosophers and everybody should be virtuous.

By virtuous he means:

- *Compulsory religious lessons in school*
- *The death sentence if you're bad*
- *Believing that the gods are incorruptible*
- *Read my books*

341 BC Greek Gazette

"STONED AGAIN"

SAYS MAN IN BARREL

Diogenes, the philosopher who lives in an old barrel, despises material possessions, and attacks dishonesty and wealth, got rough justice when he went on a stroll around Athens.

"We love dishonesty and wealth," said an Athenian, "so he's very unpopular here. Just the other day he was plodding through the streets with a lantern saying he was trying to find an honest citizen. Well, we threw a lot of stones at him. That taught him a lesson. Ran back to his tub quick as lightning, he did. Cocky beggar."

520 BC Greek Gazette

THAGS SLAMS RUDE FOOD

Colonists Knocked Sideways By Philosopher's Bean Blast

"Thags" Pythagoras has got his finger on the pulse. He's decided the soul is made of wind and so he's telling everyone: "Lay off the beans! They can damage your spiritual health."

This is the latest loony order issued in Croton, southern Italy, where the mathematician-turned-philosopher runs a cult colony.

The no-beans edict is No. 1 on a list of ridiculous rules which settlers have to obey. Others include:

- *Don't wear rings*
- *Don't look in a mirror beside a lamp*
- *Don't leave your bed unmade in the morning*
- *Don't help a man unloading freight - but do help him if he's loading*
- *Don't stand on nail clippings*
- *Don't touch a white rooster*

"Thags" is a bit of a mystery. He never writes anything down and only confides in a small circle of pals, so nobody really knows what he's saying. But his supporters claim he's still top-dog.

"His methods may be difficult to follow," said a Croton spokesman, "but they've got a purpose.

"He believes that the soul can be reborn and his rules are designed to ensure you come out well in the next life. Here at Croton we all hope to be reincarnated as kings or emperors. You other guys will probably end up as snails or beetles, and we will tread on you."

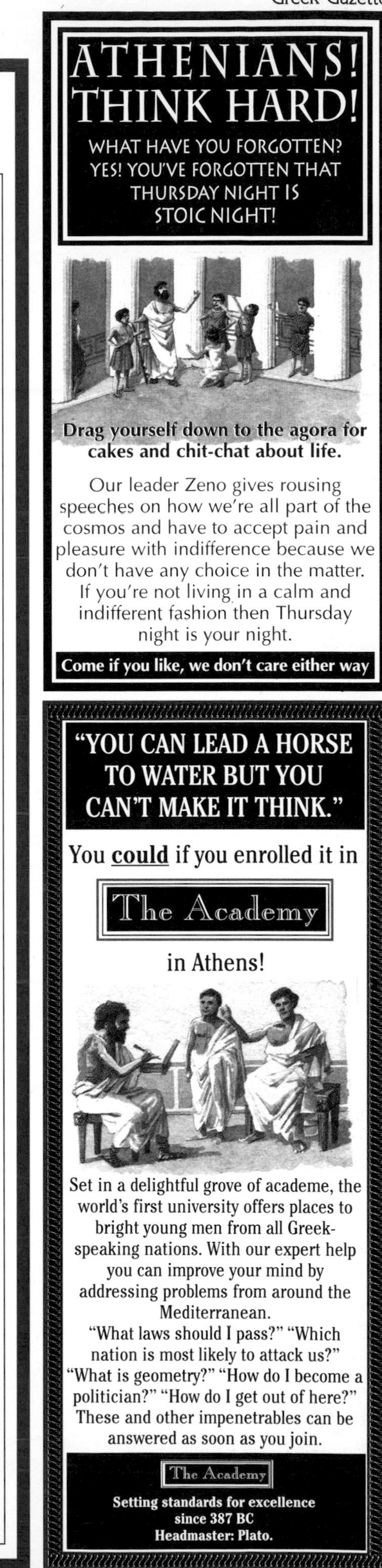

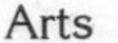

POT BLACK

NEW HUE TO-DO

500 BC

The art world is up in arms over the latest development from Athens. For decades Greek pots have been orange with black and white figures painted on them. But the Athenians have given tradition the thumbs-down. In an astonishing flight of fancy they've started producing black pots with orange and white figures on them.

"This is one of the most provocative and innovative concepts we have seen in years," said an Athenian critic. "There can be no doubt that we are entering a period of mind-boggling creativity. Centuries from now art lovers will be gazing in rapture at our pots and saying 'Truly, this was their finest hour!'"

Others disagree.

FLASH IN PAN

Peri Style, editor of *Pots and Potmen*, pointed out that, "It makes much more sense if pots have an orange background because the clay they're made of is orange. If you have a black background you merely increase your workload. In my opinion this new style is just a flash in the pan. Things will soon get back to normal."

The ordinary pot-user is baffled by the whole business. "What I don't understand," said housewife Nelly Savalas, "is why they don't broaden their spectrum. After all, it's not as if orange, white and black are the only paints available. Why can't we have purple pots? Or yellow pots? Personally, I've always wanted a magenta one with lime-green figures. Why aren't there any of those in the shops?"

Why not indeed? Let's say NO to the stuck-up so-called experts who won't use anything but black, white and orange. Here at the *Gazette* we like to encourage variety. We're offering 50 drachmas to the reader who comes up with the brightest design by next Thursday.

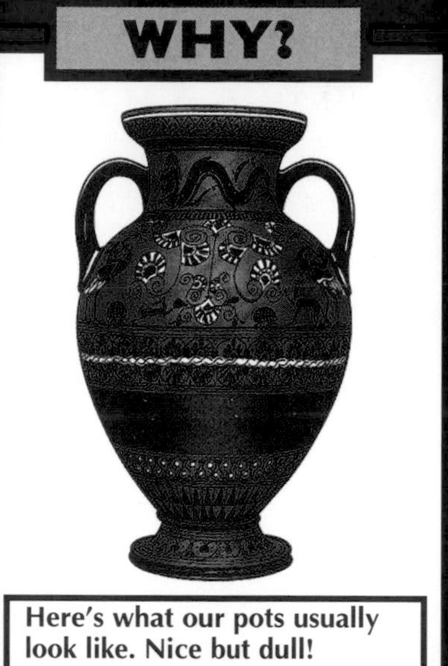

Here's what our pots usually look like. Nice but dull!

Nelly's choice. We say: "Well it certainly makes a change!"

Arts INSIGHT

THOSE SEVEN WONDERS!

YOUR GAZETTE GUIDE TO ALL THAT'S GREAT

270 BC

We sent the *Gazette* architecture correspondent on a trip around the Seven Wonders of the World. He reckons Greece tops the Google League for sheer eyes-out-of-sockets stupendosity. Here's his report.

THE COLOSSUS OF RHODES

• See this if it's the only thing you see this year. More zip than a hoplite's quickstep! A wonder in the best GREEK tradition! This one will run and run!

THE PYRAMIDS OF EGYPT

• OK if you're passing. Otherwise three big, dull, pointless pointy type buildings. Don't get out of bed.

THE TOMB OF MAUSOLUS

• Stupendous is the only word. This GREEK marvel has to be seen at all costs. Superb! Magnificent!

The Hanging Gardens of Babylon. Consistently voted "best wonder" by readers of *Slug Week* magazine.

THE TEMPLE OF ARTEMIS

• One of the best temples I have seen anywhere at anytime! Phenomenal example of GREEK architecture! Stunning! A must-must-see!

THE HANGING GARDENS OF BABYLON

•Cruddy load of pot plants. Typical Babylonian junk.Not wonderful at all. Stay at home.

THE STATUE OF ZEUS

• Massive! A towering achievement! Monumental masterpiece by GREEK sculptor, the fabulous Phidias! Beg, borrow, steal, sell your children into slavery – whatever it takes – JUST GO!!

THE PHAROS OF ALEXANDRIA

• There is no way to describe this magnificent GREEK-built lighthouse! But I'll try. Fantastic! Incredible! Left me breathless! Wonderful! Something for all the family! A tour de force! Utterly delightful! Sheer magic! Unforgettable!

BUMS ON SEATS!

CITIZENS GO STAGE CRAZY

Talk about Full House! Athens has done it again! The city that invented drama has come up with a new way of pulling the crowds – discount seating for the poor! The state has decided drama is so essential to everyday life that it's willing to pay for down-and-outs to get a slice of culture.

A packed theatre near you, yesterday.

"It's a wonderful idea," beamed one of Athens's top drama bosses. "The tickets weren't that expensive to begin with – only two obols apiece (an obol is one-sixth of a drachma, finance freaks!). But now everyone can enjoy a good afternoon out at the theatre."

"Some people are confused about drama. They say what's a comedy? What's a tragedy? Well, it's simple. A tragedy's about heroes and death and everybody cries. And a comedy's about posh people who slip on banana skins and everybody laughs. Anyway. I tell them: go and see for yourselves."

WHAT YOU THINK OF THE THEATRE

HERE'S A SELECTION OF COMMENTS BY GREEK GAZETTE THEATRE-GOERS...

- *"Fantastic! I really liked the chorus line, dancing and singing in front of the stage. Some of the comments they made!"*
- *"I loved the skene, that wall behind the stage where they paint the scenery. What lifelike forests, palaces and temples!"*
- *"The stone seats were very uncomfortable. No one told me I had to bring a cushion. But the acoustics were amazing. You could hear a pin drop. Very helpful for actors who've brought their darning."*
- *"The best part was when they hoisted that guy up with a crane and had him flying through the air to look like a god."*
- *"Great show! Great action! Great stunts! But how about a few more laughs?" (Try a comedy next time. Ed.)*

Like it or loathe it, the theatre's here to stay. And with every town boasting an auditorium – some seat up to 14,000! – attendance has never been easier!

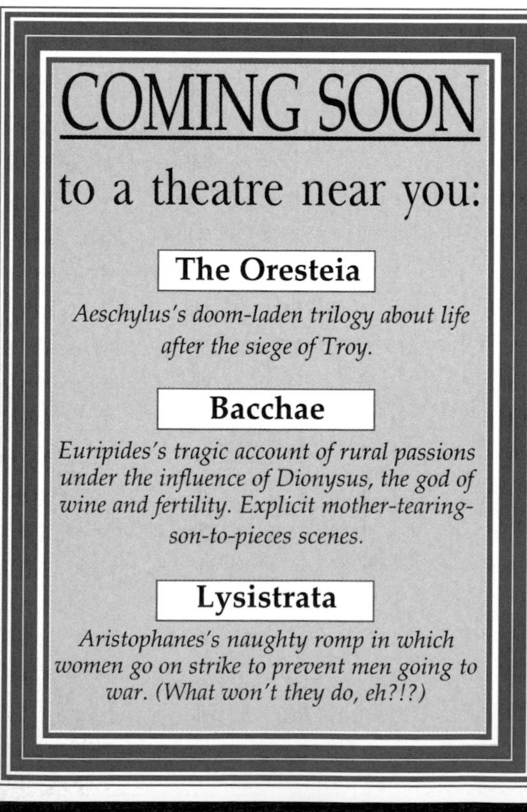

COMING SOON

to a theatre near you:

The Oresteia

Aeschylus's doom-laden trilogy about life after the siege of Troy.

Bacchae

Euripides's tragic account of rural passions under the influence of Dionysus, the god of wine and fertility. Explicit mother-tearing-son-to-pieces scenes.

Lysistrata

Aristophanes's naughty romp in which women go on strike to prevent men going to war. (What won't they do, eh?!?)

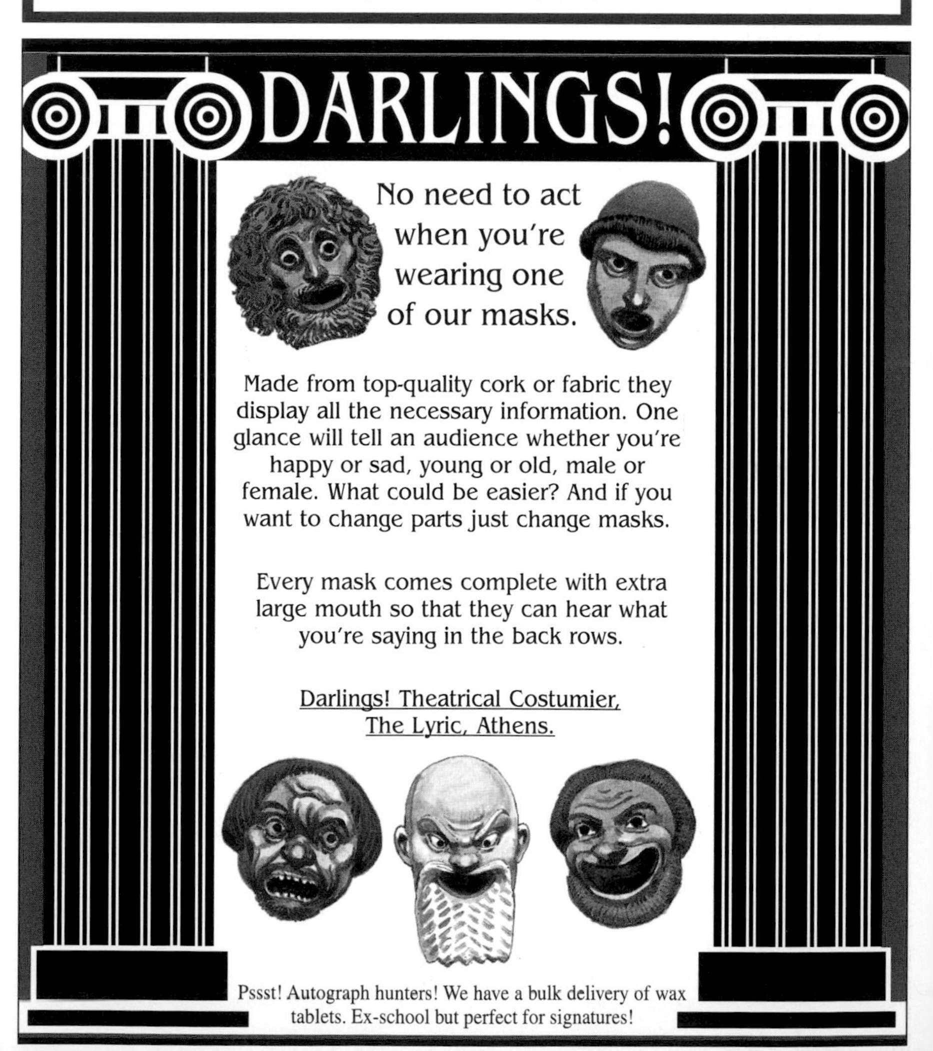

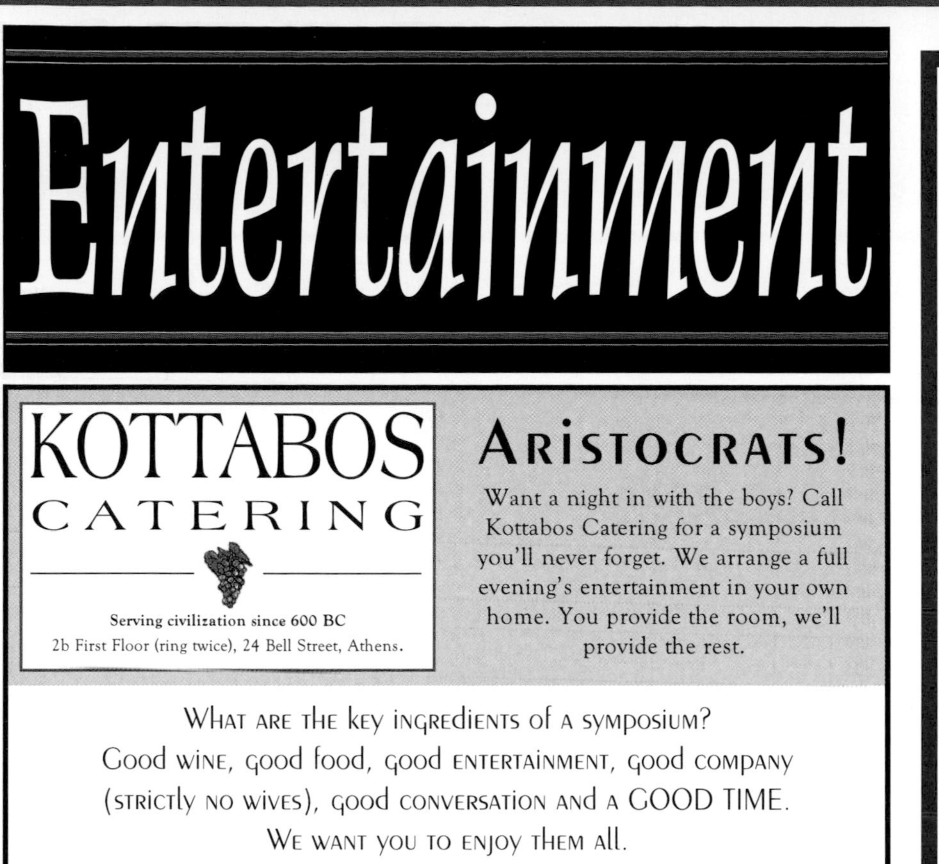

Silver Service

Our standard Silver Service includes:
Couches for 12 (2 to a couch)
Cushions Food tables Mixing bowls
Ladles Jars Cups

Gold Service

Our Gold Service has the same menu but with the following extras:
Musicians Dancing girls Sophisticated, witty courtesans from foreign lands

Menu

If you like, we can also provide food and drink. A standard meal might include:

Unlimited wine and water (mixed 1:3)
Sea urchins with olives, garlic, radishes
Tuna with herb stuffing
Meat with cheese and aniseed
Fruit and dandelion salad
Assorted cakes - poppy, linseed, sesame, honey, Eccles etc.

A butler will be on hand throughout to ensure you have the best possible time. By dawn, should any of you be unable to walk (and you shouldn't), our butler can arrange a slave service to carry you safely to your home.

BROWSERS' CORNER

MAKING A JOURNEY?

Looking for a present for Gran? Or simply lost for words? Look no further. Here's the *Gazette*'s Top Ten bestsellers. Certified to stand you in good stead for thousands of years.

1. ***The Republic*, Plato** – how to run the ideal state with only a small elite of brainboxes. Vibrant arguments, vivid imagery and practical examples.

2. ***History of Animals*, Aristotle** – what does an elephant do with its trunk? Wait and see! This is the ideal gift for nature lovers or for people you want to shut up for a while. Perfect for the beach.

3. ***History of the Peloponnesian War*, Thucydides** – eight volumes of fact-packed history. The ostracized Athenian general gives us the info on... wait for it... the Peloponnesian War! A long-journey special.

4. ***History*, Herodotus** – known as the Father of History, but some people call him the Father of Lies. Here he plies his spellbinding pen to tell us everything about everywhere. Want to know about Fiery Phoenixes and jewel-encrusted crocodiles? Then turn straight to his chapter on Egypt. A nugget of nonsense on every page!

5. ***The Anabasis*, Xenophon** – hard-hitting stuff by the one-time mercenary for Sparta and Persia, Xenophon knows what he's talking about. In this gripping adventure he relives his time as a rebel commander in the Persian army. He's better known for his previous bestsellers about farming, horses and finance, but fans won't be disappointed.

6. ***The Iliad*, Homer** – THE tale of the Siege of Troy. You'll love the bit where Achilles kills Trojan hero Hector and drags him past the city walls. A sizzling cocktail of love, heroism and revenge in the best epic tradition.

7. ***The Odyssey*, Homer** – Part II of Homer's gripping Trojan saga. Odysseus makes his way home from Troy.

8. ***Elements*, Euclid** – latest offering from the world-famous expert on maths and geometry. Popular with some.

9. ***The Frogs*, Aristophanes** – text of the belly-achingest play, from the master of comedy. Author of 40 other side-splitters.

10. ***Oedipus Rex*, Sophocles** – a heart-rending tragedy from a genius playwright. Grimace as Oedipus puts his eyes out when he realizes he's married his mother. **Urch**! Makes the best of Sophocles's most revolutionary concept – more than two characters in a plot.

HEALTH PAGE • HEALTH PAGE • HEALTH PAGE

DOC FROM KOS IS BOSS

"HE KNOWS BEST"

It's cat-among-the-pigeons time as Hippocrates, a doctor from the island of Kos, turns medicine on its head. His radical two-point proposal says:

- **Illness isn't a punishment from the gods.**
- **Doctors can cure people.**

"Before I came along," explained Hippocrates, "the medical scene was a mess. People used to worship Aesclepius, the god of healing. They'd do all kinds of stupid things, like burn sacrifices to him and sleep in his temple, so that he could visit them in their dreams and tell them how to get better. I thought, 'Nonsense! Surely there's a better way than this!' And there is."

His scientific approach to healing has made Hippocrates the main medicine man in Greece.

"My advice to doctors is this: feel 'em all over; find where it hurts; and then do something about it. Or don't, as the case may be, because most minor ailments cure themselves without interference. A lot of it's got to do with diet, so you could invent some pithy statement like, 'An apple a day keeps the doctor away.' And if none of that works, tell 'em to pray to Aesclepius.

"Most important of all, a doctor's first duty is to his patients rather than to himself. That'll be two drachmas, thank you."

"Rest the arm for a couple of days, son, and you'll soon be as right as rain." A doctor, yesterday.

Advertisement

HANG 'EM HIGH

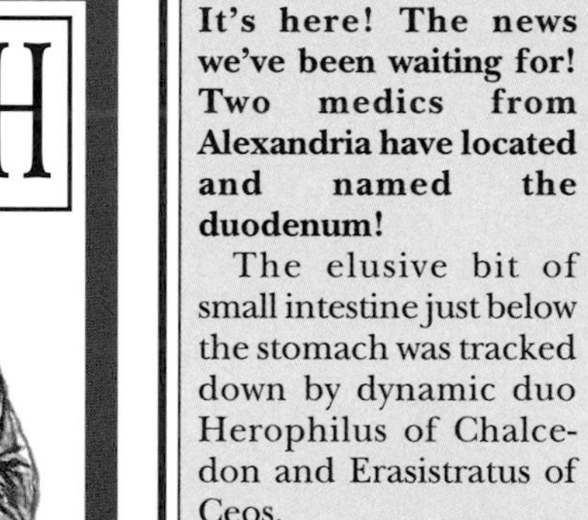

Forget the new-fangled quacks. The old ways are still the best. If you've got a problem, hurry along to a shrine to Aesclepius.

FACT: Statistically the god of healing's results are better than those of many so-called "scientific" doctors.

So why not bring along an effigy of the part of the body which is making you ill and hang it in one of our shrines. In only a few days, months or years Aesclepius will work his timeless magic.

GOTCHA!

DUODENUM "FOUND"

It's here! The news we've been waiting for! Two medics from Alexandria have located and named the duodenum!

The elusive bit of small intestine just below the stomach was tracked down by dynamic duo Herophilus of Chalcedon and Erasistratus of Ceos.

"It was nothing really," said Herophilus, whose initial research led to the breakthrough. "The thing was there all the time. All we had to do was get to it."

But how did they do it? An internal memo, leaked to the *Gazette*, revealed that the pair have developed a ground-breaking technique called cutting-people-open-and-seeing-what's-inside.

"We've discovered many important things using this method," said Erasistratus. "We've investigated the nervous system, for instance, and we've found the difference between sensory and motor nerves. Also, we're pretty sure that blood circulates around the body."

Alexandria is proud of the two docs – and not just because of their medical discoveries. Thanks to H. & E. the crime rate is plummeting.

Why? Because the knife-wielding docs only work on the bodies of criminals. And some of those criminals are STILL ALIVE!

ACHILLES: HIT OR MYTH?

NOT A BLISTER SAY EXPERTS

The autopsy is through! Mythical hero Achilles died because he was hit in the heel by a poisoned arrow.

The coroner told us:

"It appears that when the deceased was an infant his mother, a goddess, dipped him in the River Styx. (That's in the underworld, mythology fans!) The treatment was supposed to keep him safe from all injuries. In this unfortunate case, however, the mother had held onto his heel and the magic waters did not reach that part. This was only discovered during the Trojan Wars when a cunning archer twanged a poisoned arrow into his foot."

STYLE

The *Gazette* guide to what the well-dressed man and woman are wearing in the Hellenistic Period

HIM

Stylish tunic: let it all hang down if you're a senior citizen. Otherwise keep it up for maximum WOW! Lads: those legs have to be in perfect trim!

Girdle: keeps the tunic neat. Also holds in stomach if you're getting a philosopher's paunch.

Cloak: long for oldies, short for sporty, fighting types.

Hair: short and snappy does it. You don't want to have that shaggy, Archaic Period look do you?

Beard: clean chins are in! No more dithering over what length to grow your beard. Shave that face NOW!

HER

Himation: the indispensable all-over item. Two rectangular pieces of cloth joined at the shoulders by buttons or brooches, will keep you nice and warm. Make it patterned for added style.

Hair: waves and curls are IN! Pile it up. Headbands are OK but no tiaras, nets or scarves. That's old stuff!

Wrap: as fine as you can bear it. And don't forget the gold ornaments! You're after the clinging, see-through, spangled look! Forget what your mother told you about heavy materials and drab dyes. That's the Classical Period!

Jewels: stack 'em high. Bracelets, necklaces, rings – lots of gold essential.

COLONIST IN CORNISH CONTROVERSY

TRAVEL

320 BC

"I sailed around Britain – but nobody believes me!"

Wildcat explorer Pytheas of Marseilles has set the Mediterranean buzzing with an astounding story.

In his newly-released book he reveals how he sailed through the Straits of Gibraltar and circumnavigated Britain!

"What nonsense," said an Athenian admiral. "The mark of a true explorer is if he comes back with news of a fantastically profitable trade venture. If you ask me, this excitable fellow sailed into the Atlantic, hung around for a while, then came back and pretended he'd been somewhere new. If he discovered what he said he did, we want proof."

Pytheas approaches Britain. He told the *Gazette*, "Oracles say this land will become famous for appalling football hooligans, disgusting meat pies and world-class pop groups, whatever they are?!?"

"It's true," insisted Pytheas. "I landed in Cornwall then I sailed around Britain for six days. What's more I saw an island which might well be Ireland. In fact, I went so far north that the nights were only two hours long. Using the principles of latitude and longitude – invented recently by my friend Dicearchus of Messenia – that places me at 65° north.

"And what does that admiral mean by suggesting I didn't find a source of trade? Cornwall has got tin coming out of its ears. Within a few years it'll be supplying the entire ancient world or my name's not Pytheas."

While Greeks mull over Pytheas's controversial book, others are jubilant at its publication.

"We're very glad to have been discovered," said one Irish citizen. "We always thought we were here and we're delighted that an independent authority has finally recognized our existence."

YOUR POLIS

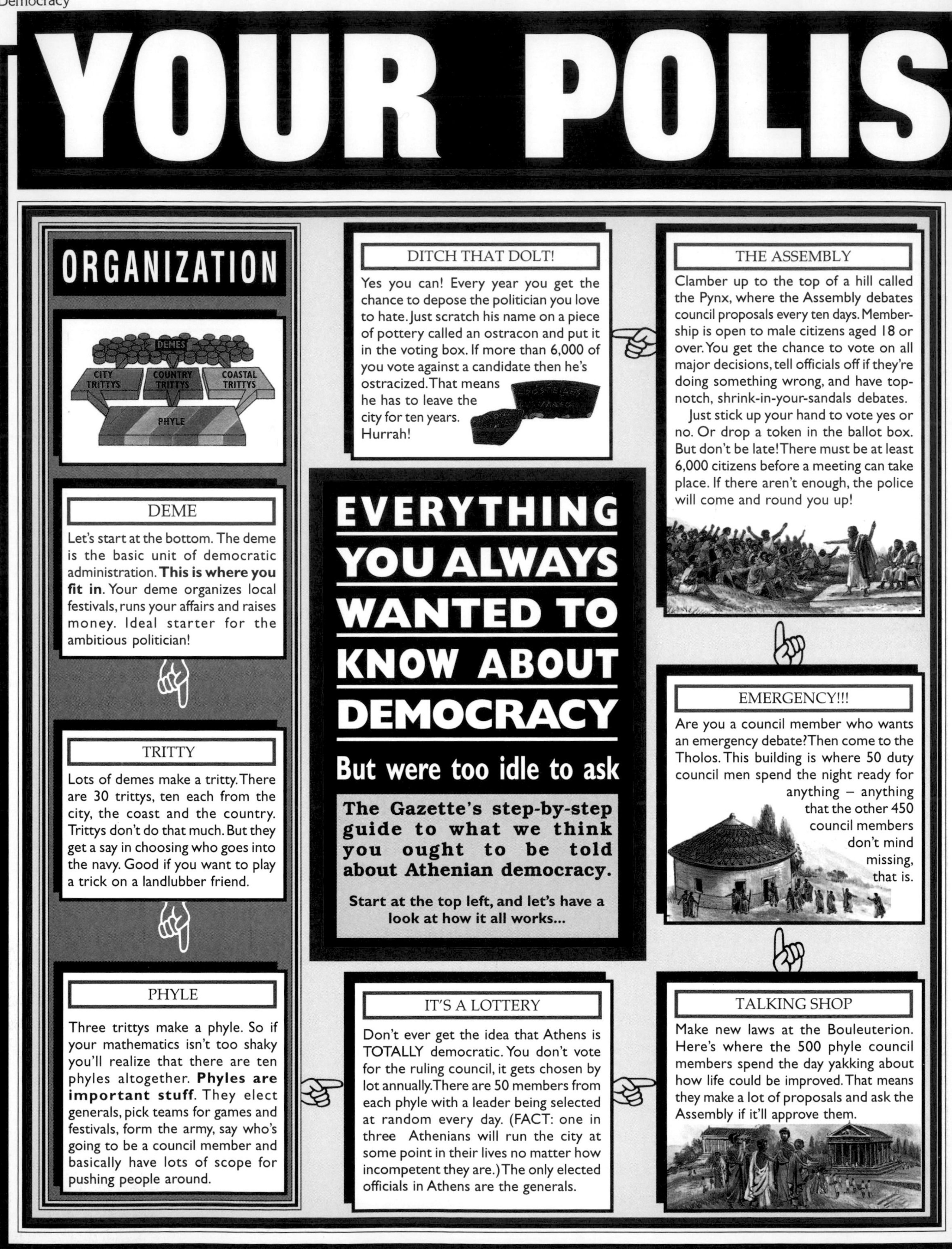

EVERYTHING YOU ALWAYS WANTED TO KNOW ABOUT DEMOCRACY

But were too idle to ask

The Gazette's step-by-step guide to what we think you ought to be told about Athenian democracy.

Start at the top left, and let's have a look at how it all works...

ORGANIZATION

DEME

Let's start at the bottom. The deme is the basic unit of democratic administration. **This is where you fit in.** Your deme organizes local festivals, runs your affairs and raises money. Ideal starter for the ambitious politician!

TRITTY

Lots of demes make a tritty. There are 30 trittys, ten each from the city, the coast and the country. Trittys don't do that much. But they get a say in choosing who goes into the navy. Good if you want to play a trick on a landlubber friend.

PHYLE

Three trittys make a phyle. So if your mathematics isn't too shaky you'll realize that there are ten phyles altogether. **Phyles are important stuff**. They elect generals, pick teams for games and festivals, form the army, say who's going to be a council member and basically have lots of scope for pushing people around.

IT'S A LOTTERY

Don't ever get the idea that Athens is TOTALLY democratic. You don't vote for the ruling council, it gets chosen by lot annually. There are 50 members from each phyle with a leader being selected at random every day. (FACT: one in three Athenians will run the city at some point in their lives no matter how incompetent they are.) The only elected officials in Athens are the generals.

TALKING SHOP

Make new laws at the Bouleuterion. Here's where the 500 phyle council members spend the day yakking about how life could be improved. That means they make a lot of proposals and ask the Assembly if it'll approve them.

EMERGENCY!!!

Are you a council member who wants an emergency debate? Then come to the Tholos. This building is where 50 duty council men spend the night ready for anything – anything that the other 450 council members don't mind missing, that is.

THE ASSEMBLY

Clamber up to the top of a hill called the Pynx, where the Assembly debates council proposals every ten days. Membership is open to male citizens aged 18 or over. You get the chance to vote on all major decisions, tell officials off if they're doing something wrong, and have top-notch, shrink-in-your-sandals debates.

Just stick up your hand to vote yes or no. Or drop a token in the ballot box. But don't be late! There must be at least 6,000 citizens before a meeting can take place. If there aren't enough, the police will come and round you up!

DITCH THAT DOLT!

Yes you can! Every year you get the chance to depose the politician you love to hate. Just scratch his name on a piece of pottery called an ostracon and put it in the voting box. If more than 6,000 of you vote against a candidate then he's ostracized. That means he has to leave the city for ten years. Hurrah!

NEEDS YOU

BALLS IN LINE? WATER CLOCKS SYNCHRONIZED? GO, GO, GO!

Or: How to work the legal system

WHO'S ON THE JURY?

Every citizen is eligible for jury service. In fact, if you're over 30 you have to volunteer. But don't worry, the trials will never last more than a day. **Plus you get paid!** Not bad for a bit of sitting around. And, since there are 200 jurors to every trial, you're guaranteed to meet some of your mates. (They say there's so many jurors to stop them from being bribed or intimidated, but we know better, don't we party lovers!)

HOW DO THEY CHOOSE?

Everybody's name is put on a card which is then slotted into a machine called a kleroteria (right). Next to the slots is a tube down which they pour little black or white balls. If there's a black ball next to your name then you get to be a juror. Simple!

WHERE'S THE TRIAL?

It's in the agora! This is where the fun starts. True, there's an official who tries to keep order, but nobody pays much attention to him. It's all up to you!

WHAT HAPPENS NEXT?

- First, a few prayers. Gabble, gabble, gabble.
- Then choose a judge from among yourselves and get on with the mayhem.
- A few witnesses will say something. (No interruptions allowed, so chat among yourselves).
- Next, the defendant will get up and make a speech. Shout him down! He's guilty! And even if he continues he only gets as long as the water clock allows him (see below). This is a device to give him a reasonable time to speak. He gets as long as it takes for the water to pour from a higher urn into a lower urn. But one of you watches the water clock, so if you're cunning you can make his speech snappy by secretly scooping water out of the top urn.

DELIVERING A VERDICT

Nothing could be easier. Each of you is given two bronze tokens. One's got a hole in the middle, the other hasn't. If you think he's guilty, drop the token with a hole into the box. If you think he's innocent drop the other one in. But keep your thumb over the middle so nobody knows how you've voted!

THEN WHAT?

Four of you count the votes. Once you've found him guilty you have to sentence him. Loadsa fun this! Choose from a wide range of penalties. For really serious violations exile is standard. But if he kicks up a fuss, tell him to drink poison. Amuse yourself by telling jay-walkers to "Drink a pint of..." (fake a coughing fit and watch them sweat!) "...rancid goat's milk!"

The information contained in this article has been selected by a show of hands among the *Gazette*'s employees in the full knowledge that the editor will fire them if they don't democratically choose what he wants.

SITSVAC

Experienced rowers required for war trireme. *Sense of rhythm essential. Must enjoy teamwork. Own oar an advantage. (Ref. GG04)*

Top oracle needs quick-witted assistant to invent pithy prophecies. *Successful applicant will have good whispering voice and experience of standing motionless behind curtain for hours on end. (Ref.GG07)*

Prestigious city Assembly is looking for competent speakers, *able to sway crowds and with good knowledge of local issues. No ranting demagogues, please. (Ref. GG08)*

Vacancies exist for sports groundsmen. *We're not very fussy. So long as you can rake sand and roll clay that'll do. Ability to drag dead boxers out of ring a help. Contact Olympic Systems. (Ref.GG09)*

Athens Odeon has part-time opportunity for rear half of stage centaur. (Ref.GG13)

Research assistant required by compilers of The Seven Wonders of the Ancient World. *Should have good sense of awe and the ability to gape. Travel allowance. (Ref.GG30)*

Halicarnassus Hoplites are always on the lookout for capable right-wingers. *If you're willing to shield the man on your left while leaving yourself totally unprotected you're the soldier we want. Naive, innocent applicants welcome. (Ref.GG37)*

PROPERTY ADS

KOJAK REAL ESTATE

We'll sell anything. No property too small. Central Greece preferred but colonies also served. Small commission. Nice staff. What more do you want?

Managing-Director Ronnie Kojak, says, "If you don't snap up these unbeatable offers you'll look sillier than a Spartan in silk stockings!"

NEW ON THE MARKET

SMALL THOLOS

This elegant little building would make ideal meeting place for city-state. Offers?

MANSION

Politician's luxury mansion. All facilities. Ostracized owner going abroad hence low price for quick sale. Don't miss it.

STOA

Fully colonnaded, with 20 shops. Vacant Possession except for one stubborn old cobbler – but they promise he'll be gone come the next dark night.

ACROPOLIS

Pillaged by Persians so decoration isn't what it used to be (neither are the buildings, to be frank). Delightful prospects. Offers also sought on surrounding area of rubble which once housed 2,000.

FOUNDATIONS

Nice set of foundations in Corinth. Lord knows what happened to the rest of it. Perfect starter home.

FARM

Delightful farm outside Syracuse. Yours for a tasty consideration.

Plenty of sheep, goats cows, grain, grapes – all the usual. All this and a sea view too. How can you resist?!?

BARREL

Freehold barrel in fashionable area of Athens. Suit Cynic or similar philosopher. All fixtures and fittings. Bargain.

These properties are correctly described at time of going to press. So buy them before things change.

KOJAK REAL ESTATE,
22 The Cypresses, Athens. Sole Proprietor: R.Kojak

CLASSIFIED

SLAVES SLAVES SLAVES!!!

For all your household needs. Top quality specimens from the Mediterranean and beyond. Write for our super-silly price list. **Fantastic discounts on ugly old men.**

"The face that launched a thousand ships." Our lovely models of Princess Helen will look perfect on your sideboard. Only three drachmas apiece, or twelve drachmas for five. ***Pericles Pots***

MARBLE

Ex-sack of Corinth. Columns, pediments, capitals etc. Daft prices. Free delivery in Peloponnese area. Otherwise two drachmas per item.

Roman Salvage and Reclamation Co.

FOR SALE

Three wrinkly olives and an old cheese.

No time-wasters

Delos Deli is taking orders for the Feast of Dionysus. Hellespont mackerel, Thessaly puddings, Rhodes raisins plus all our festive usuals. Hurry while they're fresh.

PERSONAL

Helen. Come home. All is forgiven. Menelaus. *LH03*

Want the perfect partner? Try Carbon Dating. Our unique introduction service covers all Ancient Greece. We have literally thousands of customers on our books. Call now. *LH07*

Share my barrel! Bearded philosopher seeks slim stunner to explore life's mysteries. *LH08*

I'm just an ordinary guy. I want a wife who'll stay at home all day and not say anything. Is that too much to ask? *LH09*

Have you got good ears? Tall, handsome, orator-type is looking for a wife. I talk. You listen. *LH14*

Bunnykins. Your lonely tyrant misses you. *LH28*

I know you are out there. Lady oracle would like to meet Mr. Kreosote of 10 Lymph Lane, Athens. *LH47*

You are a beautiful young girl with a massive dowry. I am a has-been Olympic athlete who once came fifth in a race. Let's meet. *LH53*

Eureka! I reeka too. Successful goatherd, own flock, seeks like-smelling soulmate for love and affection. *LH58*

Light my fire! Colossos of Rhodes would like to meet petite Egyptian effigy of Isis. *LH63*

Me Ares, you Aphrodite. Can we make the earth move? *LH68*

Comic playwright needs someone to tickle his ribs. I am author of "Why did the chicken cross the road?" and other mega-gags. You are? Send full details and a pot with your portrait on. *LH70*

Personal crisis? Contact Oedipus Introductions. We'll turn it into a drama with five acts. *LH73*

Whimsical hoplite seeks cuddly camp follower for snug winter campaigns. *LH77*

Got what it takes to make a new dynasty? Ex-Lord Of All Asia would like to meet nice Persian girl for friendship and more. *LH83*

Theban potter, 32, non-smoker, requires wife from large family of wealthy, pot-collecting aristocrats. *LH92*

Let me stamp your ticket! Elderly librarian would like to renew an overdue spinster. Alexandria-based but can travel (not very far). *LH97*

Send your replies to the Greek Gazette P.O. BOX 278

SPORTS SPECIAL

GREECE IN GAMES DISPUTE

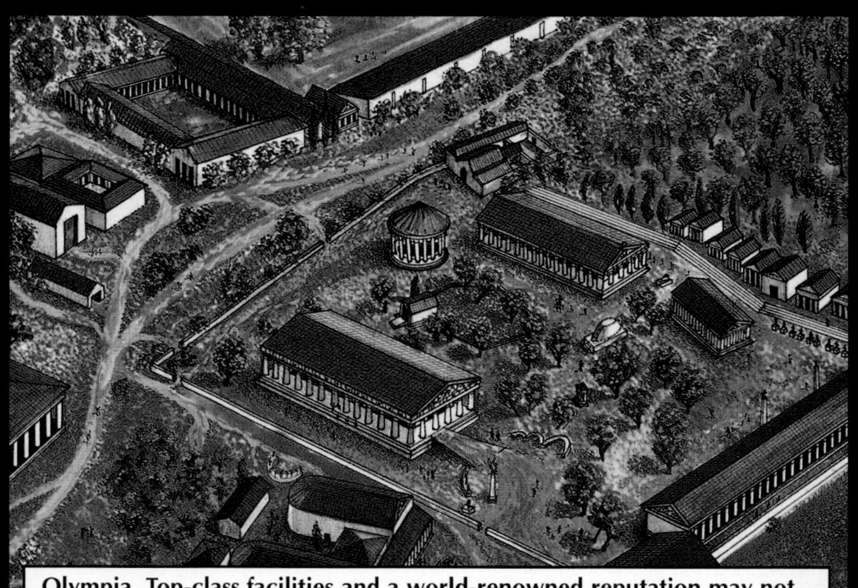
Olympia. Top-class facilities and a world-renowned reputation may not be enough to ensure the city keeps its monopoly on the Olympic Games.

NUDE ATHLETES CONFUSED

580BC

The Pan-Hellenic games are in turmoil. Ever since 776 BC sportsmen have been meeting in Olympia at four-year intervals to see who's the best. The Olympic Games have become such a part of Greek culture that everybody takes a month or two off fighting to give their men the chance to compete.

All over the Greek-speaking world, from the Black Sea to Italy, athletes have made the effort to be there.

But now there's competition. Three other cities are muscling in on the act. Delphi, Nemea and Corinth have set up rival games and officials are worried.

"This is a very serious business," said an Olympic spokesman. "The Olympic games have always set the standard. For example, ever since Orsippos's pants fell down in 720 BC and he lost the race, all athletes have competed in the buff. We've defined every single event, from long jump to discus. But now these others are trying to copy us. It's disgraceful."

CORNER

But the new games-hosts are holding their own.

"We resent the way Olympia is trying to corner the market," one Corinth senator told the *Gazette*. "We reckon that if they're going to hold games every four years that leaves three years free for us, Delphi and Nemea to stage our own events."

Each city has the backing of a top deity. Olympia and Nemea have Zeus, Delphi has Apollo and Corinth has Poseidon. So if any athlete asks "Who's going to hold it?" we say **"It's in the hands of the gods!"**

GO FOR GOLD IN THE CHICKEN RUN

THE COWARD'S GUIDE TO VICTORY

Want to win the games? Course you do. But how do you go about it if you've got a yellow streak the size of the Hellespont? Everybody knows the games are based on military skills and this makes it very difficult – to say the least – for confirmed milksops to win anything at all.

Don't abandon hope! The *Gazette* has listed the key sporting categories and has come up with some handy hints for the intrepidly-disadvantaged.

Wrestling – quite leisurely. A popular aristocratic pastime, so little danger of having your arm/leg ripped off. Still, can be quite upsetting for highly-strung types, especially if your opponent makes scary faces.

Pankration – called wrestling. BUT NOT WRESTLING AT ALL. BE WARNED. All-out, anything-goes, legalized assault. One step short of manslaughter. For psychopaths and hardened head-bangers only. Even the referee is dangerous. An event to be avoided at all costs.

Boxing – steer clear of this one, too. No gloves used. Instead you wrap your fists with hard leather straps and beat six kinds of stuffing out of each other. Ouch!

Running – no physical contact, which is a good start. If you already have experience of running away this could be the one for you. Those who usually desert with all their weapons etc. will enjoy the Sprint-in-breastplate, greaves and helmet.

Pentathlon – combines sprint, javelin, discus, long jump and wrestling. Not a bad choice. All you have to do is win three of them. Running and long jump will come easy. Of the others, javelin-throwing will best suit your battlefield experience – i.e. being as far away from the enemy as possible.

Chariot racing – perfect! Twelve hair-raising laps, 180° turns, multiple collisions, maximum casualties, dust, blood, shrieking crowds – and you don't have to do a thing! No sir! As the horse owner all you have to do is collect your prize and enjoy the adulation. (Whatever you do, don't make the mistake of entering as a charioteer.)

SPORTS SPECIAL SPORTS SPECIAL SPORTS SPECIAL SPORTS SPECIAL

ATHLETES TO GO PROFESSIONAL?

"CELERY STINKS" SAYS WRESTLER

570 BC

Winning doesn't count! It's money that matters! That's the opinion of many competitors in the Pan-Hellenic Games.

"These games can be really tough," said a disgruntled wrestler. "There's one wrestling event, for example, in which you're allowed to do anything except gouge each other's eyes out. If you do anything wrong, the ref. belts you with a stick. Then there's the chariot races. You wouldn't believe the carnage. I remember once at Delphi there was only one survivor out of a 41-chariot line-up.

"And what do you get? An olive wreath at Olympia, a laurel one at Delphi, a pine one at the Isthmian Games, and at Nemea they give you a **wreath of celery** – for goodness sakes!

"If you're a Spartan winner your 'prize' is to go in the front line at the next battle! Unbelievable!"

But sports chiefs were unimpressed. "All this glory has gone to their heads," said one.

"It's good for our city-state to come first," he continued. "It shows what a brave, warlike bunch we are and that makes everybody respect us. True, we don't pay sportsmen as such, but we do give them certain inducements to win – like rich, beautiful wives of their own choice, freedom from taxes, statues of themselves in a public place, free meals and so on. That sounds pretty good to me, so personally, I don't understand what they're whining about."

"Celery and olive wreaths are for suckers," says "Ramrod" Themistocles (right). "We want steaks and beer, and a fat bundle of cash."

KNICKERS OF FIRE

Hen-Games For Gals

480 BC

At last women have the chance they've been waiting for – a Games of their own.

"That's right!" said a Spartan housewife.

"Women aren't allowed to compete in the men's games. We're not even allowed to watch. In fact, we can't get anywhere NEAR Olympia when the Games are on."

The new festival is called the Heraia, after the goddess Hera, and it will be held every four years at Olympia.

But established athletes are already pooh-poohing it. Thirty-times-champion wrestler "Mangler" Milon of Croton said, "I suppose it's something for them to do. But it doesn't compare with the real thing. There's only one track race with three classes for women of different ages! Well, it's hardly worth making the journey, is it? They'd be better off staying at home secluded from male company, which is how all right-thinking Greek women should behave."

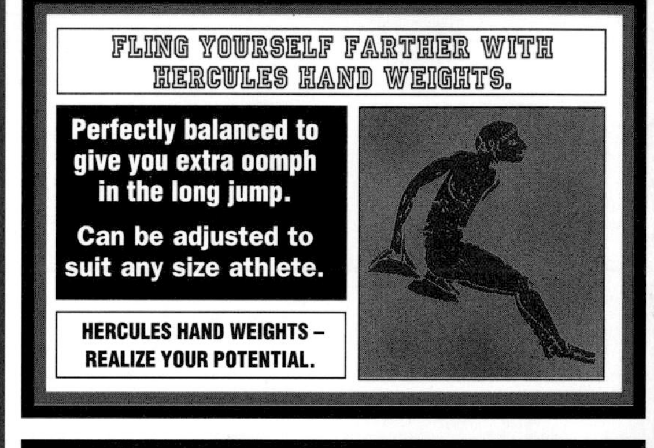

First published in 1997 by Usborne Publishing Ltd, Usborne House, 83-85 Saffron Hill, London EC1N 8RT.
First published in America August 1997

Printed in Portugal UE